# BORN FAR FROM HOME

*Paradise lies beneath the feet of mothers.*
*PROPHET MUHAMMAD* ﷺ

# Born Far from Home

## A Midwife's Search for Meaning

Shannon Staloch

Berkeley, California

ISBN Paperback 979-8-218-36827-2
ISBN eBook 979-8-218-36828-9

Cover design & illustration: Mariam Al-Quessny
Cover photograph: Zak Whiteman
Book design: R. S. Spiker, Maktaba

# AUTHOR'S NOTE

In order to protect the privacy and confidentiality of the mothers and their families, and some other people mentioned in this book, identifying names and details have been changed. All other details are true in their telling.

When Westerners encounter Muslims for the first time, they are often struck by two characteristics—their self-effacement and reluctance to project their own desires and opinions, and what naturally follows, an orientation to service in the form of true hospitality. In light of this, memoirs, with their hyper focus on the individual and her experience, are not a popular genre in Muslim circles. As a Westerner with a lifetime tendency towards insomnia, memoirs have been my late-night guilty pleasure. It is my hope that in this memoir, the reader finds not an elevation of my own story, but one that directs our focus to God and His marvelous act of life's very beginning.

The symbol ﷺ represents an invocation of God's blessings and peace upon the Prophet Muhammad: "May God's blessings and peace be upon him."

بِسْمِ اللَّهِ الرَّحْمَنِ الرَّحِيمِ

To Najeeb, for there is no book without a spine.

# PROLOGUE

In a damp, ill-lit basement of a St. Louis mosque, two men, one Persian and one Indian, are parsing the deeper meanings of a birth story. The woman in the story is alone and without her family, not even the father of the baby, to hold her hand. It's winter, and the date palms surrounding her have withered, their stems pokey and barren. The sun above her is bright but, mercifully, not hot. During the early parts of labor, contractions keep her moving, her skirt gathering dust on its hems as she paces this "place far off." The pregnancy is unplanned, and like most unplanned pregnancies, this one had moved the mother to a place beyond created forms and worldly thoughts to one of spiritual contemplation, for this life that kicked and tumbled inside her was not of her volition. In fact, inconceivably, she is a virgin.

The two men discuss whether her labor is preterm, or did the miracle of her conception also defy the standard nine months of gestation? Did she evade the lower backaches, heartburn, and pending sense of doom brought on by late pregnancy and career straight to the delivery? For she was no ordinary mother; years before conception, she could be found in constant prayer and meditation. One autumn day, her uncle Zachariah, concerned she hadn't eaten enough, brought her apples and squash, only to find watermelons and strawberries, summer's fruits, piled high on a tray. Setting his own tray down, he asked her where these unseasonal fruits originated from; she answered, "It is from God. God provides for whom He will without reckoning."

The folding chairs don't make a sound; the group is rapt as the two men move on to detail active labor. So strong is her labor that now even walking through contractions is impossible—these contractions bring her to her knees and require the concentration of her entire being. The fibers of the date palm scratch her palms and leave red marks on her cheek as she squeezes the trunk with each contraction. This is nothing like early labor! Between contractions she is cold, but during them she is hot. A metallic taste grows stronger in her mouth. She is thirsty, so thirsty.

And they just keep coming. She is no longer "her." Everything that constitutes her, her family, where she's from, her hours spent in prayer, all the physical forms of herself, are reduced to summoning the ability to surrender to the earth-shattering force of each contraction. She is no more than her breath, a contracting uterus, and the space between contractions. This unusual pregnancy, now resulting in intense pain, impels her to cry out, "Would that I had died before this and was a thing forgotten, utterly forgotten!" There is no one there to hear her cries. Another contraction, her sterling reputation no longer significant—just forget me, she asked of the world.

Before the next pain, she hears a voice in response to her cries, "Grieve not! Your Lord has placed a rivulet beneath thee. And shake toward thyself the trunk of the date palm: fresh, ripe dates shall fall upon thee. So eat and drink and cool thine eye...." It's winter. In the desert. She stares up at the trunk above her, the ends of the date fronds are shriveled, not even a bud to stir hope. Eat?!

Here the two men pause the story. The older women next to me are nodding their heads in sympathy. I've heard a version of this story throughout my life, but never quite like this.

"Will you allow me a poem in Farsi?" asks the Persian man, his stiffly pressed white shirt rumpled from the humidity. We nod in assent. As the foreign sounds roll over my ears, I look around the room. By no account do I belong here; I am the youngest person—my torn jeans, rolled at the cuff to accommodate my bike ride here, my shirt barely covering my skinny midriff all seem out of place amongst a group of women at least fifteen years older than me—black aunties in their turbans, Indian immigrants in their brightly colored *shalwar kameez*, and women from other ethnicities I can't yet place. Earlier, someone had given me a black scarf to cover my hair, and I recalled my mother having to bobby-pin a tissue to the top of her head before entering Mass.

Reverting to English, the man translates the poem, "Maryam asks God, 'Must I shake the tree to get the fruit?' 'Yes!' God replies, 'You must shake the tree to get the fruit.'" Our faith is the fruit, the man explains. Faith does not reside in declarations and belief alone; in order to reap the fruits of our faith, he goes on, we must continually shake the tree.

Maryam is birthing a child alone; yet before God offers her water, nourishment, and words of comfort, He asks her to gather

her last reserve of energy and shake the tree. It is winter in the desert, and still her shaking yields dates thudding to the ground and a spring at her feet, a miracle before the miracle.

In the basement of a St. Louis mosque, through two languages translated, Arabic and Persian, the boundaries of my own self were beginning to fissure in ways I couldn't fathom. "Hail Mary full of grace, the Lord is with Thee. Blessed art thou amongst women, and blessed is the fruit of thy womb, Jesus." The Mary of my youth, the one I would pray to in times of distress, my rosary always beneath my pillow, was nothing like this Mary. That Mary was shrouded in blue, kneeling before a manger, stoic and exalted, a feminine balm for Catholic mothers. This Mary, she had a voice and a relationship to God that I could relate to: reverent and demanding, evincing struggle and doubt, sweat and tears, and a resulting intimacy. This Mary didn't just kneel above a manger in pressed robes; she birthed a prophet in joy and travail.

In the weeks and years to come, I would continually return to her story in literal and spiritual ways. Sitting beside hundreds of women in labor, I often flashed back to Mary's story when they cried, "I can't!" "You can," I would tell them. "You're nearly there. Here, have a date and a sip of water. Don't be sad, you're nearly there." Mary's story would nurture me as well, just as it had when I was a young girl praying the rosary, only now she became Maryam, not only a balm but an exemplar seeking a direct union with God. When the weight of those morphed borders of identity and faith weighed heavy on my head, I would

# Prologue

remember the Persian poet's question, "Do I have to shake the tree to get the fruit?" Again and again the answer would prove to be "Yes, yes you do." This is a story of the date's thud.

# CHAPTER I

*She was used to walking alone and to being considered "dif-ferent." She did not suffer too much.*

—Betty Smith, *A Tree Grows in Brooklyn*

The cord has been cut. *Listen to the reed as it tells a tale, com-plaining of separation.* Blood drips from the scissors, clutched awkwardly over the medium-sized mixing bowl now cradling a deflated placenta, a temporary organ formed from the unique cells of the embryo to embed deep within the infrastructure of the maternal circulation; like a mother, this one placenta does the job of many—lungs, liver, large intestine, heart—and resembles many a mother when her children no longer need her: a shriveled balloon, spent and flabby. The new and unsure dad, his *kufi* askew, a slight shake in his hands, gaze never straying from his wife and child, returns the scissors to the midwife, who trims the cord clamp and then presses the untethered sticky baby skin to skin with its mother, hoping the hormones of the birth—still so high in this first golden hour—preserve the bond that the scissors have just physically cut.

The Persian word for *fallopian tube* is the same as the word for *trumpet*, empty on the inside waiting for a breath to sound its melody. The zygote, the fertilized ovum before division, on its slippery way down the fallopian tubes toward the rich soil of the uterus where it will dig out a foundation for the placenta, is

believed to make a cry, sounding the instrument of its mother—
for this is the soul's first separation from its Lord. *Since from the
reed bed they uprooted me.* A separation plays out in miniature as
the baby, now cradled on its mother's heaving chest, does the
impossible: a beating heart instantly dependent on lungs and the
oxygen of room air; a mouth and tongue work together, without
practice, to form a vacuum around the mother's nipple; a slug-
gish digestive system now sorts proteins, vitamins, and waste;
hazy eyes discover sight as they seek mother's face—this separation from the uterine abode also elicits a cry of separation.

We don't belong to that sleepy, watery realm. Babies dive
headfirst into the world, and this one's splashy entrance is
greeted by the Muslim call to prayer. "I bear witness that there
is no God, but God. And I bear witness that Muhammad is the
Messenger of God," whispered in the right ear by the same father
who has just cut the cord. It's baby's first clue, *You don't quite
belong here either. You belong to this mother, this father, but this
place, this isn't the final stop. You belong, and you don't.*

৪৩

On the banks of the Mississippi, in the lengthening parabolic
shadow of the St. Louis Arch, a cacophonic blues festival buzzes
its joyful and mournful notes, matching the eddies and laps of
the freshwater's flow, echoing that which I am trying to recite,
struggling to fold my tongue and buccal crevices into one Arabic
letter, *saad.* Najeeb, born in Los Angeles, the eldest son of

2

Pakistani immigrants who once taught Najeeb's tongue, formed more by English than Urdu, this very same letter.

"*Saad*. It's not an 's.' *Allahu saaa mad.*" Najeeb's mouth forms an oval, emitting a letter that sounds like a bell's gong. *God the Eternal.*

"*Saad,*" I repeat, my mouth struggling to replicate the foreign letter. Not quite the English "s" that begins on the tip of the tongue and escapes with little breath, *saad* continues to fill the cavity of your mouth like a square of dark chocolate, heavy and assertive at first, then melting into floral notes coating the tissues and taste buds as it leaves its singular mark. *Not having any equal.*

Straddling the two sides of America, mere months before 9/11, on the shores of the river every grammar school child boasts of spelling, to a soundtrack of the blues, a musical form said to have been inspired by enslaved West African Muslims who clung to these very same verses and letters, I memorize my first lines of the Holy Qur'an. *Say, it is God, the Unique.*

ℬ

In Plato's *Republic*, the well-nurtured youth is one who would "hate the ugly even from his earliest years and would give delighted praise to beauty." My own youth, a dappled mixture of both ugly and beautiful, must have had, in the incense-laden Masses of my childhood, just enough of the latter to nurture an abiding belief. I weaved my way through a typical undergraduate experience: plastic cups of beer and experimentation, backpacking for days in the canyons of Mexico, poetry slams and yoga studios, and the requisite dalliance with Buddhism. But a groundwork for God laid in my childhood judged each foray as lacking; staring into the abyss of my own self left me with a spiraling anxiety and a thirst never quenched by the lame confines of my own self-expression.

Then I met Najeeb. In his Edmonton Oilers beanie and soft smile always at play, Najeeb's gentle and intelligent presence attracts me. Working in the same coffee shop, I teach him to make lattes while he explains the fault lines of the Second Intifada. Tired of waiting for him to ask, I suggest we go for an afternoon hike in the surrounding meadows of St. Louis. On our way back, despite a full tank, he pulls over at a gas station. Looking out from the passenger seat of his Subaru, I watch Najeeb squat in a patch of grass, a plastic water bottle to his right that, between rubbing his face, forearms, hair and feet, he gently tips into his palms. The declining sun's rays stretch the shadows, and I undergo the deepest déjà vu, a cellular remembering as if I too have cleaned my body for prayer in this manner. Transfixed, I observe his wet curls and the remaining droplets falling from his face as he, without a trace of self-consciousness, rolls out his prayer mat and brings his hands to his ears, his back to the sun facing a direction proximate to where, presumably, the petrol in the tanks near him originated, bowing and prostrating as naturally as he rolls up the rug and throws it into the hatchback when he is done.

Without any explanation as to what just occurred, he slides back into the driver's seat and asks, "Should I drop you off at home?"

Mute upon observing Najeeb's ritual purification and prayer, all I can do is nod, the meaning of home has just shifted.

ॐ

That summer found my younger brother in and out of mental hospitals and me in the basement of the local mosque or sprawled under a tree in Forest Park devouring my paperback Qur'an. Our parents' difficult divorce left my brother vulnerable to hallucinations and paranoia and me searching for an enduring path to meaning.

On 9/11, I was working in an elementary school, the day's first bell had not yet rung, and the morning news was blaring on the television in the teacher's lobby. Sitting at the Formica table, preparing for a day as a teacher's aide in the special ed class, the television screen alighted with images of chaos—smoke and confusion in the streets of New York City. Scared, shocked, and unsettled, I rifled through my backpack for that paperback Qur'an, now worn and dog-eared. I needed comfort and reassurance—only later would I realize the irony of my source of succor in that moment; yet, right then, I knew unmistakably from where I was finding that pull to goodness.

Visiting my brother in a mental hospital a few weeks later, our two paths casting us further from our origins than either of us could have imagined, he demanded an answer in that edgy way of the mentally disturbed, "Shannon, why do people say Islam is violent?!"

I began a geopolitical explanation, while the one who was sick in the head wanted only an answer from my heart.

"No! How could someone say that about a faith that says about God, 'Whoever comes to Me walking, I come to him running?!' Islam is the same faith as Abraham has in the Bible, Shannon. I'm happy for you."

For so many years, my younger brother, on such high doses of antipsychotics that it caused him to walk with a limp and sleep half the day away, who still occasionally battled the voices in his head, would be the only one in my family who would look upon the decision I made to convert to Islam with anything resembling pride, and also see the path that led to it, as well as the steep path to come after. To this day, I have no idea where, deep in the bowels of a Missouri mental hospital, without internet access or a library, he could have possibly heard that hadith.

Three short months after I uttered the two sentences that are requisite for all Muslims to say in order to enter belief, the first of the five pillars of faith, I stuff what's in my second-floor studio apartment in the Central West End into a U-Haul trailer and head to San Francisco, tagging along with two friends from college who intend to live—and surf—in Santa Cruz. We take the southern route to avoid the Rockies' winter weather, dipping down through Oklahoma and Texas, tracing Route 66, ascending the San Gabriel mountains as wide-eyed, awestruck, and hopeful as the Joads when they too encountered California. We arrive in Berkeley in the early evening—the lights in the hills sparkle, their charming constellations a compass confirming I have arrived at my destination. *I will never tire of this view.* The thought, both a command and a plea, is a seedling, its tip beginning to burrow beneath the moist California soil, a root sown before the U-Haul is even unpacked.

დ

In *Islam and Secularism*, Syed Naqeeb al-Attas, a contemporary Muslim philosopher from Malaysia, compares the Westerner's concept of knowledge with that of a thirsty traveler, who at first sincerely sought the water of knowledge but soon found it plain and so salted it. The traveler now drinks incessant cups of water, his thirst never slaked, and his original need to drink forgotten. In St. Louis, Najeeb had loaned me a DVD set entitled *Foundations of Islam*, a course taught by an eloquent and erudite man named Hamza Yusuf. Minutes into watching the eight-hour series, I tasted my first brineless cup of water. I came to California to drink more of that water.

Shaykh Hamza, as he is commonly known, accepted Islam as a teenager after a near-death experience and studied for years in the Muslim world, acquiring a mastery of Arabic that enabled him to learn Islam's liberal arts tradition and classical texts in their original language with, among others, a notable tribe of Bedouin scholars in the remote deserts of Mauritania, before returning to California to teach and translate the tradition to Western Muslims, most of whom are *ajami*, an Arabic word meaning "mute" but generally referring to a person whose mother tongue is not Arabic.

On a few acres of serenely undeveloped land tucked away almost out of sight in an otherwise gritty part of the East Bay, Hayward, just south of Oakland, a few structures sit in a grassy field at one of the vertices of a wedge-shaped property: a classroom, a small bookstore, and a green canvas yurt. These constitute what was then called Zaytuna Institute. Shaykh Hamza envisioned Zaytuna as a place to teach Islam's traditional texts as they have been taught for much of its history, a teacher conveying the knowledge encapsulated in a text to students in an unbroken chain of teachers that links back to the Prophet Muhammad—pure water to thirsty Western Muslims.

The classroom is unfurnished except for thick red Afghan rugs and rows of burgundy BackJack floor chairs. Wooden teak partitions, carved with arabesque patterns, divide the room into men's and women's sides. A small platform, draped in the same Afghan rugs, rises in the front of the room, set up for a teacher with a small floor table and chair.

I take a seat on the women's side, next to the divider. Above me float chattering, happy conversations, while children skirt the floor chairs, tipping water glasses and earning glances of disapproval from their elders. Ittar, the scented oil worn by Muslim men and said to attract angels, permeates the rapidly filling space. Everyone settles on the floor, at the foot of the awaited teacher, ready to play their part in this chain, this ancient transmission of knowledge.

Shaykh Hamza strides into the classroom and instantly the chatter quiets, his presence felt before either seen or heard. Seating himself on the platform and clearing his throat, the turbaned shaykh begins, "Salam alaykum. Audhu billahi minash Shaytan ar-rajim. Bismillah ar-Rahman ar-Rahim...." He continues for what seems like forever in a string of Arabic lost to my untutored ear. But soon he is off and running in English—the entire lecture, "The Rights and Responsibilities of Marriage," is woven of the two languages. Beginning with the chapter of the Qur'an entitled "Rome," we traverse Islamic history from its earliest days to the Mongol invasion of Muslim lands, shifting to the metaphysical signs encased within masculinity and femininity, to the nature of attachment, and then to marriage as an institution.

Pens scrawl about me as the women in class take notes on the rights granted to wives in Islamic law beginning in seventh century Arabia. I learn that when a woman works, her earnings belong to her, while her husband remains financially responsible for providing food, clothing, and shelter for her and their children; anything she spends of her own earnings is considered charity. She's also not required to do housework or cook; instead, she can include a cook and a housekeeper in her marriage contract, and even request compensation for nursing their baby for up to two years.

This is not a dusty prayer hymnal at Mass; this is a guidebook taught by a guide. It's knowledge not for the commerce of this world but for the trade between this worldly life and the next. Shaykh Hamza's class opens a cupboard door to a dizzying world of Islamic beauty and sensibilities. I unexpectedly find myself an heiress to gems and riches, to spiritual giants of past times I had never known existed but whose unfamiliar names—Imam Ghazali, Imam Malik, Ibn Arabi, Imam al-Haddad, among others— would soon roll off my tongue as if they were close relatives.

Despite not quite having the lingo (what is the difference between *alhamdulillah* and *masha'Allah*?) or the uniform of flowing skirts and robes, each Saturday, in my vintage jeans and thrifted sweaters, I return. In between classes, I listen to recorded lectures in my studio apartment in the Berkeley Hills. I can't get enough. Islam is an ocean, and, once underwater, I have little need to come up for air. Soon, I am known by name, not my last name yet, but at least by my first. And I begin to learn the first names of others, including Fuchsia, Nabila, Cynthia, and Kamila, with whom I will find not just friendship but inspiration—for they are the first women I encounter who have birthed their children at home with midwives.

ॐ

In Yelena's office a different type of community is forming, one of mothers and fathers, gathering to educate themselves and venture outside the thick red lines that guard medical orthodoxy to choose an out-of-hospital birth. Her office, midway between Santa Cruz and Silicon Valley, attracts a patchwork pool of clients—independently minded ER doctors, techie Silicon Valley singles pregnant via IVF, hippie herbalists and back-to-the-landers, even the rare Bay Area evangelical Christian, all seeking a birth away from the managed care that hospitals sell.

Yelena becomes my first midwifery teacher, though our chain is a broken one. California stopped issuing midwifery licenses in 1949, severing the transmission of knowledge for generations of women. Yelena's home office is off Highway 17, the route that winds twenty miles southwest from San Jose to the coastal town of Santa Cruz, where decades earlier, in the spring of 1974, federal and state agents conducted a sting operation against three local midwives. Dressed in ridiculous hippie gear, beads, and bell-bottoms, federal agents posed as a couple in labor desiring a home birth. When the midwives showed up to the faux birth, they were told the laboring woman was in the shower; when they walked to the bathroom to check on the woman, agents swarmed in from the surrounding redwood trees and arrested the midwives. The sting began a court battle culminating in the California Supreme Court case *Bowland v. Municipal Court*, which established state restrictions over parental choice in childbirth options; while the midwives' attorneys attempted to use *Roe v. Wade* to invoke a woman's right to choose as a precedent for her right to choose *where* to birth, the state court decided that—in this case—the rights of the unborn child superseded the right of the woman to choose. Midwifery would stay underground until the late nineties, just years before I ended up in Yelena's office, relinking the broken chain.

Yelena is a midwife from the pages of every seventies book on birth, with her long salt and pepper hair and hazel eyes that captivate with a mirth unique to watching the miracle of birth thousands of times. She wears a lot of purple. Every year, she takes a couple of weeks off to visit her shaman in the rainforest.

She makes me feel at home right away. "Hello, Shannon! The water is hot, and there are lots of teas to choose from. Pour yourself a cup and let's chat!"

As I pour a cup of ginger tea, I look around at the pictures of the families on the walls, most of them beaming from their beds, half-dressed, with a post-birth glow. "I'll bet you will find some familiar faces up there," Yelena chirps. "I'm sure I've delivered many of your friends!" I didn't know she had even noticed my religious affiliation, and for once, I have forgotten about it, but she is right: there are Nabila and Nejma, two of the women whose families I had come to know at Zaytuna. The connection relaxes me even more.

Here in Yelena's office, the transmission of knowledge isn't formal; we sit facing each other on two worn couches, and within minutes what I think is an interview becomes an overview as Yelena details the expectations she has of an apprentice: clinic days in office twice a week, four to six births a month, and in-home postpartum visits every other day for the first week post-birth. I am drinking this water in, too, a blossoming knowledge of Allah's most spectacular act of creation.

Yelena teaches her childbirth education classes to expecting parents one night a week in the same office—these, she tells me, are optional to attend but an excellent way to gain a deeper understanding of her philosophy. I'm up to the task—although, I discover, birth has a way of laying bare our similarities and our differences, of which there were many on both sides.

ℰ

One night, I attend the childbirth classes that Yelena teaches. It's the last in a series, so naturally, she's arrived at postpartum and newborn care. After reviewing different breastfeeding positions, Yelena shows a video.

"I want you to see what a circumcision actually looks like, and how awful and cruel it is for the baby," she explains as she slides in the DVD. There is a baby, strapped to a board and alone on a table with only a bare bulb hanging above. The doctor enters with a gown, gloves, and a scalpel. As he stands over the baby, he makes an initial cut, and the baby screeches. The wailing continues for the full seven minutes of the video. You'd have to be a monster (or a Muslim or a Jew) to consent to circumcision after that.

The lights come back on, and Yelena scans the room; most of the mothers, in full pregnant bloom, are wiping away tears and clutching their partners' hands. "Can you see how violent a procedure this is? Muslims and Jews are the only ones who still do this regularly," she asserts authoritatively. "And just look at how violent their societies are!" Apparently, the debacle in the Middle East was not due to corrupt governments or land disputes but to circumcision. Fielding what I perceive as sidelong glances from the expecting couples, I want to crawl in a hole or, at the very least, yank off my hijab. I was admittedly politically naïve, but I was learning, yet nowhere in my reading had I come across circumcision as a possible cause of the Palestinian-Israeli conflict. As soon as class is over, I slink out into the dark, cool evening to lick my wounds and consider the miniature clash of civilizations that just occurred.

It's unsettling to be unceremoniously grouped with people you're only just getting to know—and, simultaneously, to be disassociated from those you thought you knew. I understand the feeling of not quite fitting in; in my own splintered and regrafted family, with step- and half siblings often at the center of each of my parents' new lives, it wasn't unusual for me to feel sidelined. This time, though, I experience it on an unfamiliar geopolitical scale that strips away something larger about me. I entertain the impulse to retreat into my new and burgeoning Muslim community. I could exist only there, a sort of spiritual refuge blissfully protected from people horrified by circumcised penises, but I also know that I need Yelena to teach me skills the Muslims cannot. I would have to get used to being an other, the dizzying experience of being all too visible yet frequently invisible.

෮෮

Carrie is a Christian and carrying her ninth pregnancy. Her mild temperament attracts me. Frizzy waves of hair flow past her waist. A bright-yellow summer dress, chosen for its modest cut, barely conceals her ballooning belly; she has weeks to go, yet it looks like she could push her baby out this afternoon in Yelena's office. Still, her body shows signs of wear. She winces with each step. Pubic symphysis pain emerges when the small joint between the two front pelvic bones loosens and wobbles. Carrie feels the painful tug on her pelvis with each step. In labor this little bit of extra movement provides the give her baby needs to descend, but in pregnancy, it can be excruciating. Carrie doesn't complain, though, as she carefully maneuvers around the pain and climbs up onto the exam table, pressing her knees together as she moves from sitting to lying.

Yelena palpates her belly, feeling first for the back of the baby, and then sliding her hands toward the pelvic rim to check for baby's head. "Are you hoping for a girl or a boy?" she asks Carrie before turning to me. "This one will be the tiebreaker, Shannon—Carrie has four of each!"

Carrie laughs. "We are happy with what God gives us, but another girl would make me more than a little happy." We hug goodbye at the door, and Carrie looks at me and says, "Shannon, it was great to meet you. I'm looking forward to having you at my birth." Not sure why, I feel relieved and grateful. On my ride home, I marvel at how I thought gaining midwifery knowledge was about rubbing backs, taking blood pressures, and swaddling babes, but these moments are more than that—it's like sitting at the feet of the shaykh: it requires not just your head but a pure and steady heart.

❧

Weeks later, I am reading in bed when the phone rings. This is pre-iPhone midwifery, so I walk into the living room to answer it, shivering in the night's chill. "Shannon, Carrie is in labor, and we have to move fast. She lives in the Saratoga mountains, and you will not be able to MapQuest it. Meet me downtown Saratoga at the parking lot of the Big Basin Café. You can park your car there and ride with me."

Barely processing Yelena's stream of instructions, I change my clothes and head out into the night. It's pitch-dark and not a single car passes through Saratoga's upscale downtown. Yelena's blue BMW with the license plate TOBIRTH—in case there is any doubt about where we are headed—is parked, engine running, as I breathlessly clamber in. She flies through the curvy mountain roads without even consulting a map. I am nervous and withdrawn, grim warnings from my assorted midwifery texts fluttering through my brain. A multiparous woman has a higher risk of hemorrhage: her uterus, spent from birthing so many children, can give up after relinquishing the baby and fail to contract sufficiently to clamp off the blood vessels. As we drive deeper and deeper into the mountains, we distance ourselves from immediate medical care. I am running through how to handle a hemorrhage—angelica tincture, shepherd's purse tincture,

Pitocin intramuscularly—and finally the picture of bimanual compression pops into my head: one gloved fist inserted into the uterus to tamponade the open blood vessels, the other hand pushing down hard from the top, doing for the uterus what it is not doing for itself.

Yelena seems serenely oblivious to the notion that an emergency can arise. "It's the house with the big, white mailbox. On the right—yes, here it is!" She swiftly turns onto a gravel driveway, which leads to a sprawling white farmhouse, a kitchen light softly glowing from within. We sweep in through the back door, leaving the screen open to let in a cool breeze for the laboring mom—who is, in fact, laboring in the kitchen. Not only has she chosen the kitchen, but she is laboring in a stainless steel horse trough filled with water. Instantly, any thoughts of bleeding vanish from my mind. This is good. This is normal. It's another day on the farm.

Yelena and I say hello, and Carrie smiles her big, open smile at us before closing her eyes and settling deeper into the warm water. Her husband gives her a sip of water. Carrie's large farm kitchen is clean and crisp, revealing no traces of the family of ten's dinner from that night. Yelena decides to set up the birth equipment in the adjacent hallway—a heating pad warms the receiving blankets for baby, an oxygen tank stands ready nearby, a small kit of medications to control hemorrhage lies next to the pouch of sterilized birth instruments. Sterile and non-sterile gloves are stacked at the ready. As I am taking note of how Yelena likes her setup, I hear a whistling from the other room. It's a soft and low whistle that comes every few minutes, lasting for about a minute. I peek my head into the kitchen and see Carrie, pursed lips and closed eyes, whistling through her contractions! I smile in disbelief, and Yelena, by her side for seven of these nine births, tells me she always whistles through her contractions.

Soon, Carrie wants out of the water. We towel her off as she makes her way to the rocking chair in her room. We spread a chux pad beneath her and drape a towel over her. Again, she whistles, now combining it with rocking, every contraction a whistle and a rock. I know labor is progressing by the strength of her whistles; they become more forceful and high-pitched, and before long, the whistling turns to grunts. "Get ready," Yelena says, "this part is going to go really fast." I grab a few receiving blankets off the warmer in the hallway and place them against my skin beneath my shirt to keep them warm. Carrie continues rocking, whistling, and grunting, as her husband holds her hand. She scoots progressively closer to the edge of the rocking chair, tilting her pelvis up toward the ceiling, naturally following the ancient instructions her body already knows. Yelena and I are observers of the oldest miracle, mute at its immensity.

But Carrie's husband is not. "Jesus, bring this baby safely into its mother's arms! Make this baby a righteous baby! Fill this baby with Your love, O Father!" He prays ceaselessly and loudly. On one hand I am comforted, and on the other I am holding my breath that he doesn't slip in a prayer for my heathen soul.

A big contraction washes over Carrie—it's too strong for a whistle or a rock, and all she can do is arch back and push. In one push emerge dark hair, shoulders, amniotic fluid, and a lusty cry—the miracle is complete. As Carrie gathers her baby up into her arms, the cosmos settles back into place, and our voices slowly return. I remember the blankets beneath my shirt, and tear one off to begin gently warming the baby.

"Thank you Jesus, thank you Jesus, thank you Jesus," Carrie repeats while giving her baby a once-over. She lifts the blanket. "It's a girl!" she announces with teary eyes. My own eyes shift to the chux pad between her legs as I remember the seed of fear that I had on the ride here. Yelena, too, intently watches. There is little bleeding, and soon the placenta slips out almost unnoticed. Crisis averted. "Thank you, Allah," I say to myself quietly.

The next day is warm and sunny. Making the drive in the daylight reveals a narrow two-lane road flanked by towering redwoods and sparkling creeks. The horse trough is emptied and drying on the wraparound porch. I find Carrie nursing her baby in their homeschool room: chalkboard walls, antique desks, a rocking chair, and reams of sunlight. I wonder if she will be as comfortable with me, a Muslim woman in her home, now that she's not in the throes of labor. Her proclivity for and ease of religious expression make me nervous, as if I were playing dress-up with my new faith and just realized the clothes were too big. I'm sweating.

19

Carrie sets down the book she's holding. I ask her what she's reading. "*A Tree Grows in Brooklyn*. It's my favorite book of all time. Have you read it?"

"No, what's it about?"

I listen as she tells me about Francie, the child of Irish immigrants growing up in Williamsburg, Brooklyn, often ridiculed for her family's eccentricities. It seems a world away from here. Carrie, in her telling, has to pause every so often as her uterus contracts in an attempt to shrink back to its pre-pregnant size, a painful cramp that goes by the simple name of *afterpains*. For a mother of nine, this is a feat. Five bottles of herbal tinctures, which Carrie squirts in her mouth with every cramp, sit on the side table next to her.

"These are the worst—so much worse than the labor pains!" I'm paging through her chart, wondering what exactly I'm supposed to be asking her about. She's done this nine times more than I have. My inexperience, combined with my unnerving self-consciousness about quite possibly being the only Muslim to ever set foot in her house, flusters me. I fall back on taking her blood pressure. It never hurts.

As I am fumbling with the Velcro on the cuff, securing it around the arm not holding baby, I flash her a nervous smile, a mask to my insecurity.

"Your teeth are so white!" she exclaims.

I look at her, startled. Just last week, in another world at Zaytuna, Shaykh Hamza had related a parable: Jesus and his companions once passed by the carcass of a dog. One of the disciples said, "What a foul stench this dog has!" But Jesus responded, "How white are its teeth!" Jesus, in his gentle way, was training the tongue of his companions to say only what is good, even at the sight of a dead and decaying dog carcass.

I look at her again, this time with more assurance. For all my insecurities about the unfamiliar religious roles I have played in the past weeks—me as the backward believer who circumcised; me as the unredeemed interloper into the confident Christian's home—a simple postpartum visit has shown me that the prayers Carrie's husband expressed weren't much different than the ones I had whispered earlier that day, except that I cupped my hands and he folded his. But in a world increasingly defined by disbelief, we both pray. Our differences, understood another way, can point us past our mere identities, past denominational and credal fault lines, to our Creator.

Here in this Christian home, nine children are bending toward what is beautiful and away from what is ugly—to see the white teeth of a decaying carcass, not the stench. Muslims have a name for this inclination to goodness, *fitrah*, which all children regardless of creed are born with; it's the lifelong journey of a Muslim to protect and return to this primordial state.

"One hundred and ten over sixty-eight. Perfect," I tell her as I roll the blood pressure cuff up with renewed confidence.

"Can you squirt the herbs in my mouth?" She grimaces as her hands are tied up with her baby and her uterus continues its work of involution—of returning to its original state.

# CHAPTER 2

*Do they not see that God brings life into being and reproduces it? Truly this is easy for God.*

—Qur'an 29:19

I'm pregnant. I know it without peeing on a stick or peering at an ultrasound screen. It's spring and the buds bloom without instruction, and that simple truth jumps from my blooming uterus to my face, and I cannot stop grinning. Or dry heaving. There's also a pesky urinary tract infection and a rapidly developing anemia. But before the embryo becomes a fetus, I'm sure it's a boy and we've decided on a name: Salek, after the Mauritanian shaykh teaching at Zaytuna who married Najeeb and me, and because it means "spiritual wayfarer," a traveler in the world and one who travels on a path to the divine.

Renee, our midwife, makes house calls. I don't have to leave my one-bedroom apartment, with high ceilings and shoji window treatments that soften the South Bay sunshine, in San Jose's Japantown, for prenatal visits. We have one couch and lots of makeshift floor seating. I sit on the couch and Renee sits on the floor—charts, paperwork, and a fresh pot of tea dot the coffee table in front of her—this seating arrangement will become routine as the pregnancy progresses. Regardless of her luxury car or expensive clothes bought in San Francisco boutiques, Renee prefers the floor and our chipped teacups. We adore her.

"Renee, I'm leaving next week for overseas. I'll be gone for three weeks. I'm a little nervous about the nausea, and I don't know what kind of food they have there, so I don't know how well I'll be eating. Is there anything I should watch out for, or do while traveling?" My teaspoon clinks against the side of my cup long after the sugar has dissolved, ringing across the room. I'm a jangle of nerves and nausea.

"Where are you going?"

"Mecca." It's Renee's turn to stir the tea long after it's sufficiently sweetened.

"Mecca! Wow! Well, it will be hot so you have to be sure to stay hydrated and to stay cool and not overheat. Try to avoid processed foods and sugar." Clearly, she has never been to the Middle East. Neither of us knows what to expect.

Similar to midwives, who view their profession as a calling, one doesn't *decide* to go to Mecca and visit the Prophet in Medina; one is called to the holy cities by God.

ℰℴ

One night after arriving in California, I heard that there was an open mic for poets that a few other young Muslims would be at, so I brought a dog-eared notebook of poems that only other early twenty-somethings would snap to and headed to the theater. Knowing very few people in the crowd, I read a poem I had read in St. Louis many times before, only this time in hijab and with a shakier voice. California is always the bigger stage.

Afterwards, I was getting ready to leave when I heard a boom-ing voice, "Sister!! Masha'Allah! I need a copy of that poem!" Usama Canon—cool, fashionable, and self-assured—strode across the room and proceeded to recite a couple of lines from my own poem back to me. Usama came to Islam less than five years before I did and was nurtured in the shade of Zaytuna and by the many scholars who visited. He also traveled to the Muslim world, quickly learning Arabic to a level advanced enough to al-low him to teach. Managing to stay rooted in the Northern Cal-ifornia culture that raised him, he appeared to lack any of the dislocation that I wrestled with. I'd reflect later that men who convert to Islam have an easier time remaining cultural chame-leons than women, who convert with the same zeal but often feel compelled to pull the hijab across their hair to visibly mark their conviction.

Our families became instant friends; he plays chauffeur for our honeymoon, when Najeeb and I travel south to San Diego's turquoise waters, not to swim and relax on its sandy shores in our swimsuits but to hear lectures and attend the gatherings of a visiting Muslim scholar from Yemen, Habib Ali al-Jifri. Our honeymoon would be spent fully covered in mostly gender-seg-regated gatherings.

Leaving San Jose at night, Usama opens his trunk for us to put our suitcases in, pulling out a gun to make room. Before our gaping mouths, and with the ease of a seasoned chef slicing on-ions, Usama deftly removes the ammunition and separates the gun into halves. "I have a license. As long as the weapon and the ammunition are in different parts of the car, it's legal," he reassures us. Not even a year after 9/11 and with a driver by the name of Usama, we are packing heat down Highway 5.

The stars come out and we settle into the long drive, one of three cars of seekers from the Bay Area. Usama puts on some jazz. As we hurtle down the highway, hearts eager to soak up anything of this precious new faith, I feel the melding of the two sides of myself—a pilgrimage down a highway accompanied by jazz. When the light rises over the Tehachapi Mountains on the Grapevine, the entire caravan pulls over and makes *wudu* from plastic gallon bottles of distilled water. Someone calls the adhan, and three lines of travelers pray the dawn prayer.

At our first stop on the lecture tour—a Los Angeles suburb— I take a seat in the living room with the men I had traveled with before I'm promptly asked by the host to relocate to the kitchen or upstairs, with the other women, out of sight. Usama looks perplexed: he sees both sides of the dilemma, the need to respect the visiting scholar from a conservative Muslim country where women cover their faces in public and to placate the new American convert who will surely take offense to such an ask. However, through the God-given gifts of his particular temperament and personality, Usama performs the alchemy that can happen when the best of both worlds meld. The result can be a balancing act, often off-kilter—the Islam too foreign, or the American too laissez-faire—but Usama was adept at walking that tightrope without losing balance.

Behind the semicircle of men, a loveseat is pushed against the back wall. Usama spies it out of the corner of his eye and says to our host with utter conviction, "She's going to sit right there."

For the rest of the gathering, I sit alone on the loveseat and watch as the semicircle enlarges with men and as the women who enter, gathering their long skirts and robes, keep their gazes straight ahead, and ascend the stairs to their designated room.

I feel mannerless and out of place; had I gone straight upstairs, I would have fumed at the request, but staying downstairs, the only woman amongst men, also proves uncomfortable.

❧

So, in order to move from the periphery, I am going to the center. Now eight weeks pregnant, I board a plane to Saudi Arabia. By the time we land in Cairo, I am thoroughly disoriented. Out the window of the plane all I see is brown: brown buildings, brown runway, brown cars, even the air looks brown. Nothing looks familiar anymore, not the people, the words, the script, and the disorientation manifests in huge waves of nausea that I tame with a bag of Jolly Ranchers and cans of Sprite. I want to turn around and go home. Why had I thought I was up to the challenge of traveling so far without my husband, while newly pregnant for the first time?

Our group arrives in Medina around midnight. We pass an exit sign that would appear unremarkable on the freeways of California; but this one, rather than indicating the street you would find upon veering off the freeway, delineates two exits: one for non-Muslims and one for Muslims. The ancient idea of a walled city contrasted with the familiar green and white exit sign makes me feel as if I am entering a place otherworldly yet enduring.

A simple green dome, erected in 1818 while Medina was under the governance of the Ottoman Empire, marks the resting place of the Prophet Muhammad ﷺ. Today the mosque and its courtyard dwarf the original size of the city. Gigantic umbrellas open and close shading the varied pilgrims that flock here from every corner and byway. Once I enter the mosque, I feel as if I am in the presence of a generous king, the air is remarkably cooler, the hard marble floors shine beneath my bare feet—barefoot and pregnant is regal here. I drink hundreds of paper cups of Zam Zam, the holy water sprung from the heel of Abraham's son Ishmael; its minerals become the building blocks of the unborn child coiled in my belly: Sprite, Jolly Ranchers, and water from the ancient well of Zam Zam.

Iranians dressed in turbans and crisply pressed robes mingle with West Africans in their flowing boubous and Afghans in their wool shawls atop dignified strides. The local Arab women dress in their version of an LBD—little black dress—an ornately embroidered and highly bedazzled, floor-length black robe with bell sleeves; it trails behind them as do their many children and more often than not a nanny from the Philippines, while they hold court in the mosque serving small cups of Arabic coffee and dates at sunset, their generosity extending back rows and rows—

surprisingly, they always seem to get all of their dainty glass cups back.

୬୨

The windows are open to let in St. Louis's paltry summer breeze, and I can see the stars twinkling from my perch in the tub. Muslims, whose holy book was revealed with the command, *Read*, tend to revere books and language; rarely will they leave a book on the floor, and if one is found there, especially one with Allah's name, the infraction is quickly rectified with a kiss to the book's cover. This humid night in St. Louis, though, occurs months before I learn the manners accorded books. So, I begin reading *Muhammad* by Karen Armstrong. After months of reading about Islam, I am convinced of the first part of the declaration of faith: there is no God worthy of worship but God; the second part, that Muhammad is His last and final Messenger, I am wrestling with.

Belief in a prophet that isn't in the Bible feels like the final step outside of my family's faith. I really want to know who the Prophet Muhammad is, and why belief in him is so necessary to this faith I am growing toward.

A few pages in and I am transported to the warring clans of seventh-century Arabia. Due to the hard Meccan winter rains, the Ka'aba had fallen into disrepair. The clans of the noble Quraysh tribe, the caretakers of the Ka'aba, were responsible for its upkeep. The repairs were humming along until it came time to decide who would place the final stone, the Black Stone, into the structure.

Muslims believe that the Black Stone fell from heaven to Mecca during the time of Adam and Eve. Worn smooth by centuries of caresses and kisses from Mecca's pilgrims, the Black Stone sits in the Eastern corner of the Ka'aba. The clans of the Quraysh tribe began to argue amongst themselves over who would have the honor of placing the stone back into its niche. Reaching a fever pitch after four or five days of unsuccessful negotiations, this could have meant war. Preparations for a battle were being made.

Then, the eldest man there had an idea. He proposed that the next person to walk through the sanctuary's gates would elect the clan that would replace the Black Stone. Crickets chirped outside my window, and the bath water cooled; my senses heightened as I kept reading. The elders of the clans waited with bated breath, praying that the soul who came through the gates would honor their clan. Hours later when they saw who it was, all the clans rejoiced.

"Al-Amin!" they cried with relief. The Trustworthy One, a name Muhammad was known by. My eyes filled with tears. When Muhammad walked through the gates, the clans could think of no one more trustworthy. With great calm and intelligence, Muhammad took off his shawl and directed the men to place the stone in his shawl. A man from each clan, he said, should grab a corner of the shawl, lifting the stone up, so he could place the stone back into the eastern corner of the Ka'aba.

In that eureka moment, I accepted the second half of the testimony of faith: Muhammad is the Messenger of God.

Archimedes discovered the principle of displacement while in the bathtub: the volume of water displaced is equal to the volume of the body immersed in the water. All the emptiness of the impetus to find the truth via my own feelings, to carve my own way to the truth through only the whims of the self, sank in that moment, displaced by knowing the Best of Creation. God didn't leave us without a blueprint; he left us with a trustworthy guide, al-Amin, so perfect in his humanity, that he displaced the rest of creation and the paltry ounces of our own selves so that we could float and not sink.

ॐ

To be Muslim in a place where there are only other Muslims is a door opened and a foot firmly planted.

It's also to look back home and see the distance traveled.

After a few days of adjusting, the sense of displacement that had crept up on me in Yelena's office has met me in Medina. I am feeling especially out of water as I look around. It seems the people in my group are having real spiritual experiences. They spend hours with their palms upturned in supplication, reading page after page of the Qur'an that stutters and stops when I read it, slowly sliding my finger beneath the looped letters, like a first grader reading phonics. They deftly sling prayer beads between thumb and forefinger with litanies I am unschooled in while I nurse my nausea, not feeling particularly spiritual.

On our last morning in Medina, I walk alone into the mosque, moving as close to the Prophet as I can go. The women are crowding and shoving to get as close as they possibly can to his blessed resting place as the female guards in face veils shout in Arabic to move back, seemingly blind to the love that propels us forward. I find a clearing and sit down, away from the claustrophobia of the crowd, when I hear singing. A group of Iranian women, in their chadors, are gathered in a circle next to me holding small books, their soft voices rising in harmony and drifting up toward the green dome. I imagine the Prophet  himself hearing their melody and smiling, his face round and lit like the full moon, teeth a perfect string of polished pearls, content with their songs of praise.

These women are not singing in Arabic; they are singing in Persian—their foremothers were like me, tongues tripping over Arabic letters, newcomers to a religion that had once been a stranger in their lands. The music did what my brain could not: it grabbed my heart and carried me outside myself. Their notes of longing expressed my own, their melodies infused my doubts with fresh faith, and sitting alone in that small spot in the Masjid an-Nabawi, surrounded by Turks, Arabs, Indonesians, Nigerians, and more, a young woman born in the middle of America found a piece of home. I let the music of Persia carry me away.

જી

BORN FAR FROM HOME

Back in San Jose, my belly is pulling my clothes tighter by the day, and the rubber band I use as a makeshift maternity pant expander can't stretch any further. At our next prenatal, I tell Renee that I'm antsy to get back to my midwifery studies.

"You should go to Casa de Nacimiento in El Paso," she offers. "I went when my youngest was four."

Casa is a high-volume birth center where women come from all over Mexico to deliver their babies on the Texas side of the border, guaranteeing their children birthright citizenship in the United States. For a student apprenticing in an average-volume home-birth practice, it can take up to five years to acquire the clinical numbers needed to sit for midwifery boards. The lack of pay and irregular hours can be challenging for many young students starting their own families, so they often opt to spend some time at a high-volume clinic like Casa.

"Is it safe to go while pregnant? Won't it be hard? What about the lack of sleep?! I hear the twenty-four-hour shifts can be grueling for non-pregnant students." I feel excited but nervous at the prospect.

"It will be hard," she says, leaning over the coffee table, "but it will be harder to sit on this couch with a newborn, knowing that you have so much further to go. Stick some trail mix and carrot sticks in your pocket, and sleep on your days off. You'll be fine."

32

Renee's years of mothering and midwifing are boons to my understanding of what balancing motherhood and midwifery may look like.

And with that, for the second time this pregnancy, I am off. I've brushed up on my Spanish and pored over midwifery texts. I am ready for a month of attending births in Texas, a world away from Mecca and Medina. Twenty-five weeks pregnant, I fly into El Paso in November; as I look out the plane's window at the rust-colored Franklin Mountains against the cerulean sky, I wonder if I am physically and mentally ready to scale the mountain of this midwifery clinic for one month, adding one more personal challenge to this pregnancy.

The faces of the expecting Mexican women light up when they see my belly. "How far along are you? Niño o niña? El nombre de tu bebé? Are you going to have it here?" I laugh and tell them that I am the one who is supposed to be asking the questions. Despite the difficulty of their journey to the clinic—a wait in long, hot lines at the border between Ciudad Juarez and El Paso, where they are frequently turned away, causing chaos in our appointment calendar; sometimes missing work and leaving their other children with friends or relatives just to come to the clinic for the two prenatals required by Casa to deliver on this side of the Rio Grande—I see only smiles and never hear one complaint.

During the day, we do *citas,* or prenatals, in a sparse room with only an exam table and some posters in Spanish on the wall. There is a thin paper chart for each woman, and a significant language barrier; we get by with my four years of college Spanish and their rudimentary English, which we usually lean on more than my Spanish. I take blood pressure, palpate baby's position, listen to fetal heart tones, measure uterine growth, and record it all in their charts—if we are lucky, there is lab work from their doctors in Mexico to thicken their files.

One young woman, Erica, comes in at regular intervals and almost always on my shifts; with her wide smile and carefree manner, we connect over the elation and uncertainty of carrying our firstborns. She's curious whether I'm nervous about the pending labor. Of course, I tell her, and watching all these births isn't helping! On one of her last visits, I take her blood pressure and note that it is elevated, at 152/95.

Hypertension in pregnancy can be a symptom of a dangerous condition called preeclampsia. It can also be a problem on its own: constricted blood flow in a mother means her body is working double time to simply move blood while also nourishing a growing baby and an extra organ, the placenta. Babies born to mothers with high blood pressure can suffer from intrauterine growth restriction, weighing in much smaller than another baby born at the same gestation. The placenta is also at risk; placental abruption, a true obstetric emergency, occurs when the higher pressure shears the placenta from the uterine wall, cutting baby immediately off from its only oxygen supply. It can be said that monitoring a woman's blood pressure is the sole reason for pre-natal care. Once it's found elevated, we need further lab work to determine the cause.

"We cannot take you as a patient with high blood pressure," I explain to her in my limited Spanish. "It is dangerous for you and the baby. If you cannot make your appointment next week for us to check it, you will have to see a doctor in Mexico and bring us the lab work."

She nods and says she understands and promises to check in with the doctor. We proceed to listen to her baby's heartbeat with a Doppler; my own baby thumps against my belly to the sound of her baby's heartbeat. I tell her, and she reaches out a hand to my belly. My baby kicks back in greeting.

ℰℒ

It's not my shift, but I am in the clinic to chat and soak in the nightly excitement of babies arriving. I see Erica's name on the board, and I ask the midwife what happened with her blood pressure. She said that Erica had seen her doctor in Mexico and the labs looked good. The midwife asks if I would like to attend her birth even though it's my night off—I run to change into my scrubs.

The birth rooms in the clinic were decorated in the eighties and never updated. The floral pastel wallpaper matches the ruffled pillow shams and stuffed teddy bears. The full-size, four-poster wooden beds are covered with a thick rubber mattress protector. There is a rocking chair in the corner, perhaps meant for nursing, but most often occupied by a concerned grandmother, auntie, or sister.

Erica had arrived in active labor and is progressing quickly. Laboring while standing, she places her hands on the wall and sways her hips during each contraction. I wonder what her journey here was like. Was she able to lean against a wall while waiting in line at the border crossing? Did the women waiting help her, offer a sip of water, a word of encouragement? I turn to introduce myself to her husband.

"Congratulations! It's nice to finally meet you. My baby and yours are already friends!" I tell him during one of Erica's contractions.

As Erica catches her breath she tells me, "That's not my husband. He wasn't allowed to cross the border. That's my brother-in-law."

*Her brother-in-law.* I'm incredulous. She crossed an international border in labor, with only her brother-in-law to accompany her. I think of my own brother-in-law back in California and cannot imagine laboring with him in the room.

Since I am technically not on the shift, I excuse myself for a quick dinner and reassure her that I will be back as soon as I am finished. After dinner, when I return to the room, the mood has changed. Erica is on the bed, her back propped up against the pillows. Her brother-in-law sits stiffly next to her, unsure where to look or what to do.

Normally, one student and one staff midwife attend each birth, but now all three students on shift and both staff midwives hover and kneel around the bed. Standing in the doorway, I have

36

an unsettled feeling that propels me past the crowd to Erica's side.

Putting my arm around her and my mouth close to her ear, I whisper, "Respiro profundo—buen trabajo," as I glance at the furrowed brows and tight lips of the circle of midwives and students around the bed.

One of the students places the Doppler just above Erica's pubic bone. Rather than the galloping horse hooves of a vital baby on the brink of birth, there is a feeble, intermittent heart rate— *boom…boom…boom…*water dripping from a leaky faucet. Time slows to match the pace of the baby's struggling heart; we are a tableau of every mother's worst nightmare, desperate midwives and a mother straining against fate to deliver a screaming infant into the world.

Watching the impossible feat of skull bones sailing beneath a pubic arch, I can lose faith in the process: this baby isn't going to squeeze out of that miniature space. *It won't work,* I tell myself. To witness birth is to consider its opposite, death, and the life after.

ॐ

At night between shifts I read a book by the great eleventh-century philosopher and theologian Imam Abu Hamid al-Ghazali, *The Remembrance of Death and the Afterlife.* Ghazali, who is to Muslims what Saint Thomas Aquinas is to Catholics, uses the Qur'an, the life of the Prophet, and sayings from the pious to describe in evocative detail the moment the soul departs from the body, the trials of the grave, the physical resurrection, and the soul's final and eternal resting place, Heaven or Hell.

Again and again, the skull bones of a newborn mold and overlap to accommodate the impossibly tight space of a mother's pelvic bowl. Ghazali emphasizes this act of birth as a moment for the believer to reflect on what she has just witnessed. "How can one who has seen that such a thing lies within the bounds of His creative ability and power deny that resurrection is within His capacity and wisdom also?"

As a Catholic, all I knew about death was the waxy, familiar fingers of my deceased grandfather folded atop his lifeless chest and my grandmother's bland promises that he was in heaven now. Ghazali doesn't use such banalities or reassurances. He details the forms in which the Angel of Death takes souls—if you are a sinner, the angel adopts a form that makes even the prophets faint, but if you are a soul heavy with piety and good deeds, the Angel of Death appears in the form of a young and perfumed handsome man; in the case of the especially righteous, he is flanked by thousands of angels holding rods of sweet-smelling basil and forming two rows as they escort the soul back to its Lord.

∞

"Es una emergencia, Erica. Empuje, muy fuerte!" I tell her. Someone hands me a pen and paper and asks me to chart the times, but all I can do is whisper urgent directions to Erica. Midwifery is not yet imbedded in my brain; its unique rhythms and their deviations, a cue to sit up and note the time's passing as it relates to vital signs. I am new to the forest and have yet to orient myself to the particular trees and wildflowers of the landscape. It is all heart now. I am an expectant mom at the bedside of a mother birthing a compromised baby; we are sisters on the path of motherhood and I will not leave her behind. Charting the time of this birth belongs to lesser gods. I set the pen and paper on the nightstand.

"We see the baby's head! Good job, mama! With the next contraction, push the hardest you have ever pushed!" yell the midwives. I peer over Erica's bent knees to see the baby's crown. Rather than a head flush with blood and squished like a raisin, this baby's skull is a dull and ominous gray. The midwife takes a gloved finger and runs it over the top of the head, hoping to stimulate the heart rate. *Boom*…a single rock tossed into a pond.

My blood turns cold with horror, and I instinctively reach down to feel the familiar contours of my own baby who kicks in response. I feel the beginning of a sort of survivor's guilt, for I can see that shortly ahead, Erica's and my paths are diverging. I grab her hand, smooth back her hair, and reorient us to the work ahead. For now, we are walking together.

"Amiga, todo esta bien, pero necesitas empuje muy fuerte para tu bebé." Over and over, I am coaching her to push with all of her might. After three interminably long pushes, the baby arrives in a bath of meconium and silence. The midwives spring to action, one holds a stethoscope to baby's heart. "Twenty," she calls out, as in twenty beats per minute. The other midwife performs CPR while a student rushes to call 911. Meanwhile, the baby, pale and without tone, is unresponsive.

Erica lets go of my hand and pushes herself up to sitting, reaching for her silent baby. The midwives swat her hands away and my stomach curls into knots. It seems cruel to deprive the baby and the mother of each other. As soon as she sits up, Erica feels a cramp similar to a contraction. *La placenta,* I tell her. The midwives and students are busy working on the baby, so it is up to me to deliver her placenta. Unceremoniously, the placenta plops into the bowl. Erica is no longer pregnant.

The paramedics bring only an adult-sized stretcher, and the baby looks like a washed-up doll in a sea of yellow netting. Erica sits up, defying anyone who tries to quell her as she reaches for her baby on the stretcher leaving a trail of fluid across the room. Upon seeing the inert body of her baby, Erica, who has just spent time in that liminal space between life and death, knows before anyone else that her baby has not crossed the threshold with her. What God gave her for nine months, He has already taken back.

Her cries are guttural and elemental, the soul-penetrating, unmistakable sounds of a grieving mother. The paramedics move quickly while Erica's brother-in-law restrains her from walking out of the room after them.

"Mi bebé! Mi bebé! Ay Dios mío, mi bebé! Oohhhh, mi bebé! Dios mío!" Her hands, which she had used to push herself up from the soiled bed, leave bloody prints all along the faded floral wallpaper. Most women have trouble sitting up so soon after birth. Erica, infused with superhuman strength, rails at the cold hand of fate. No one has the heart to stop her.

I slink against the wall to catch my breath, trying to process the events that have transpired, and to reconnect with the living baby inside of me. The room expands; I imagine there is a whoosh of departing wings and a lingering scent of basil.

ഇ

Days later we learn that Erica had visited a doctor in Mexico, where they too had found elevated blood pressure, but rather than schedule the appropriate testing, or even an induction, they had prescribed her diuretics, pills that masked the blood pressure and hence allowed her to proceed with our clinic, thereby granting her baby the opportunity to be born north of the border, to manicured lawns and backyard pools and one day, perhaps, a better life. It crushes me all over again.

How desperate, then, must be the situation of some women? So desperate that even trained medical doctors are willing to take known dangerous risks with the lives of mothers and babies? My vision of a water birth in my living room feels like the ruminations of royalty. Sipping tea with Renee, a privilege reserved for the elite. My baby's kicks, an hourly benediction.

Erica's and my paths did diverge. But Ghazali explains the future junction of our paths:

It behooves the man whose child or kinsman has passed away that he should treat his antecedence in death as though it were a journey in which his child has preceded him to a country which is his dwelling place and homeland. His grief will not then overwhelm him, as he knows that soon he is to catch up with him and that there lies between them nothing save an early and a later departure.

Although our destination is the same, her child will precede us there. He will wait for his parents, in the paradisical nursery with the souls of all the other departed children. The tears of this terrible afternoon will become eternal joy for Erica. Islamic tradition states that on the Day of Judgment, a stillborn or miscarried fetus will drag both parents into Paradise by its umbilical cord, the very same cord I just cut. The cord, a lifeline for babies in the womb, is now Erica's lifeline for eternity.

A midwife stands at the threshold of life and death. Returning home, I realize that beyond the skills I have gained, this fact is precious knowledge. Just as I had to travel East to find my place in the West, I had to learn that death is on the other side of this precious effort to birth life.

# CHAPTER 3

*All the diversity, all the charm, and all the beauty of life are made up of light and shade.*

—Leo Tolstoy, *Anna Karenina*

I did not plan for my water to break that cold January morning, just three weeks shy of my due date and one day after my own birthday, but before I'm even out of bed to wash hands, face, and feet for the pre-dawn *fajr* prayer, I hear a pop and feel the unmistakable warm gush of fluid that for the past nine months has cushioned the limbs of the baby, who, it seems, I will soon be cradling in my own limbs. I pray before the sun rises and go back to a soggy, sound sleep.

At about noon Renee comes by to check on the baby's heart rate, which plots out like a steady but jagged line indicating good variability, a heart ready to handle the squeezes and compressions of labor. Renee deposits a kiddie pool, or more accurately for today's usage, a birth tub, a key feature of my pain-relief plan, now an exotic plastic island amongst the mundane furnishings of my living room. Before leaving, she inventories my birth supplies: gloves, bendable straws, a cord clamp, gauze, and adult diapers for the postpartum bleeding.

"It's all here," she cheerfully chirps, "but there's no food. You will need food to keep your energy up throughout the labor. As do your midwives! Why don't you and Najeeb walk down to the grocery store this afternoon and pick out a few things that look good to you? I'm fine with bagels and cream cheese. Even if your contractions start coming while you're out, it's fine, stop wherever you are and breathe through them, then continue with your walk. It will be a good distraction!"

In his encyclopedic *Muqaddimah*, Ibn Khaldun, the fourteenth-century Arab historian often considered to be the father of sociology, includes an entire section that he titles "The Craft of Midwifery." In order to coax my baby and prime me for the upcoming birth, Renee charts a course that her midwifery colleagues have followed for thousands of years; her fluffing of my nest, her attention to the baby's heartbeat, her encouragement to distract myself and eat in early labor, and her emphasis on quality over quantity as labor nears—a bright demeanor and decided absence of cervical checks or predictions of the length of time until baby arrives—all serve to settle my nerves and ground me in the physical work of what's to come. Ibn Khaldun defines midwives by this skillfully subtle attention: "Midwifery is a craft that shows how to proceed in bringing the newborn child gently out of the womb of his mother and how to prepare the things that go with that."

৪৩

My grandmother Elaine was the second oldest of fourteen children. She was born in 1929 to my great-grandmother Olive in a farmhouse in southern Minnesota, where the next eleven children would arrive under the care of the same family doctor who also diagnosed their measles and quelled their coughs, until the birth of the youngest nearly twenty years later in the hospital with a new doctor, this time an obstetrician, nearly one hour's drive from her home. Now one year into midwifery school, I had attended about twenty births, nearly all of them resembling Olive's first thirteen births, the majority taking place in living rooms, kitchens, and often the very bed on which the child was conceived.

Birth in America has only recently moved to the hospital. At the turn of the twentieth century, nearly every American birth took place at home in the presence of both physicians and midwives. As early as the 1930s, only half of all American births, usually of rural, immigrant, or African American women, happened out of the hospital. However, despite birth moving into the hospital, the number of infant deaths from birth injuries had increased by approximately 50 percent in that same time period, and the maternal mortality rate had not budged.

In less than one hundred years, American midwives and the craft they honed, along with the particular, commonsense knowledge of birth they possessed, were entirely obscured from obstetrics, leaving doctors to rely heavily on often dangerous medical interventions, like episiotomies and forceps, and the drug scolpamine, otherwise known as twilight sleep, which dulls the pain of labor but does not render women unconscious, a nightmarish experience, where a woman can feel pain but is unable to express any discomfort. Gone was the simple advice to take a walk and eat, along with the knowledge of the emotional and physical signposts at each of labor's stages.

The historian Wendy Kline writes about Dr. Joseph DeLee, one of the most influential obstetricians during this period, who graced the cover of *Time* magazine in 1936 as "the best obstetrician in America." His textbook, *The Principles and Practices of Obstetrics*, went through thirteen editions, and his invention for clearing the airways of newly born infants, the DeLee, named after him, is still carried in the birth bags of many American midwives. Although he also invented forceps, which contributed to the rise of medical interventions in birth, he himself benefited from, and encouraged his students to attend, home births, stressing to students the importance of observing an entire labor, not just parts of one during a shift, and one not muddied with medical interventions, as the premier way to understand birth. "You learn all the physiology of childbirth and you have to know that and know it well before you can really apply your obstetrical knowledge and manage and deliver a baby properly," he exhorted his students.

Had DeLee and his students observed my labor, they would have noticed this laboring mother's need to eat. By the time Najeeb and I walk to the grocery store, I am famished. We stop at a local college pizza hangout, and I order two slices and a huge Sprite (the lemon-lime drink accompanies me throughout this pregnancy!). By the time I am done with lunch, I feel my first contractions and rather than the dread or anxiety I was silently anticipating, I am giddy and relaxed. I want to meet myself on the other side of labor. Wandering around the grocery store, I notice the contractions pick up in strength. I stop at every other aisle end, leaning into the weekly specials, to breathe and sway through the tightening sensations. Unbelievably, as we are carrying the bags back home, I feel hungry again! What is this impetus to eat? I'm the Very Hungry Caterpillar from the children's book, eating and eating and eating until I spin a cocoon around myself, and a butterfly emerges.

ℬ

After another nap, the moon has risen and the sun has fallen, and my uterus, like the tides of the ocean, is not oblivious to these facts, producing stronger contractions that propel me up off the bed, hands on the wall leaning over, a position I'd observed mothers frequently adopt in labor.

"What's for dinner?" I ask Najeeb after a contraction, as I blink in the living room's light.

"Dinner?! You're still hungry? I thought laboring moms didn't eat?!"

He makes hamburgers, and between contractions, I devour two.

Satiated for now, I am bouncing on the purple birth ball in front of the laptop as it plays the Qur'an's chapter of Maryam, her birth story echoing from its tinny speakers, the rounded Arabic script a contrast to the sharpness of contractions that grab

47

me, forcing my chin to my chest and my hands to my knees to steady me as I roll my hips in a circle, the ball turning beneath me.

"Oooooopppppeeennnnn. Oooooopppppeeennnnn." I chant through each contraction, elongating each consonant and vowel, the vibration of my voice traveling to the tight, unexplored crevices of my body. Every muscle needs to relax or the sensations become almost unbearable. Yet once the contraction is over, it's gone, a mirage of sensation. Between contractions, the Qur'an's cadence fills my ears, and my eyes read the translation.

"So eat, drink, and do not grieve…."

In a hospital, I would have been denied the opportunity to eat and drink, the rationale being that if I were to need an emergency cesarean section, the food in my stomach could be aspirated into my lungs, potentially causing aspiration pneumonia. There would be a needle in my arm attached to an IV bag, my only nourishment for the duration of labor, its pole on castors, requiring the coordination of every hip circle not only with my breath and vocalizations but also with the tethered IV. My throat and mouth dry from vocalizing, I would be allowed only ice chips, rather than a glass of water, to quell my thirst.

Had DeLee's students observed me in labor, they would have garnered the wisdom of the Qur'anic advice to eat and drink, perceiving that laboring women have the caloric output of a marathon runner, their need for food and drink essential during one of the peak physical performances of their lives. The keenest students would have discerned the hospital policies to deny laboring women food or drink as a setup for a tired mother with a weakened uterine muscle to require pharmaceutical augmentation of her labor with a drug called Pitocin.

So far, nothing has impacted this labor other than the rising of the sun and its setting. It's hard and focused work that requires stamina, and the mental mindset of a long-distance runner and a Robert Frost poem, "But I have promises to keep, / And miles to go before I sleep…."

Najeeb takes my labor in stride. As my mantras of "open" increase in intensity, he asks, "Shannon, don't you think we should call the midwife?" I had only been having contractions for a few hours at this point, so I insist not yet. I'm afraid of having the midwife come too early and in my limited experience of birth, most first-time mothers have days of labor. He trusts my experience over his observations, proceeding to kick his feet up on our couch and lose himself in the latest issue of *The New Yorker*. It is a scene equivalent to the proverbial midwife knitting in the corner, and I am comforted by it.

The labor, demanding more and more of my concentration, leads me to pause the Qur'an, as the hard work of what I'm doing prevents me from giving attention to its verses. I move to the recliner, hoping that form follows function, and recline while shutting my eyes between contractions. With each contraction, though, I must sit upright, my bottom scooting to the edge of the chair as I place my feet flat on the floor to help me rock, back and forth, back and forth, back and forth, my intonations of "Ooooopppppennnn" in step with my rocks. When it's over, I sink back into the corduroy upholstery and fall into a dreamless sleep, only to be woken by the ferocity of my contracting uterine muscle.

Shaped like an upside-down pear, the uterus responds to labor contractions in two different ways. The upper, rounded portion of the pear responds by thickening, never relaxing completely even between contractions, while the lower segment, the stem side of the pear, is more passive, contracting with less intensity, thinning and opening as labor progresses. The retraction of the upper uterine segment is akin to bunching up the fabric of a turtleneck, so the opening, or lower segment, enlarges. This is cervical dilation.

When I feel nauseous, I begin to wonder how far dilated I am and how much longer I can go on. I know that if I were in a hospital, refusing an epidural would require enormous commitment at this point. My request for a bowl and a cold washcloth rouses my husband. The bubbles of more Sprite ease the nausea, but I'm feeling hot and cold, uncertain. "I'm calling Renee," Najeeb decides. At this point, labor is women's work. He's out of his league.

It seems to me that she is at the door in ten minutes, but I know her drive from the coast to my house is forty-five minutes. When she sees me, I notice her pick up her step; there's urgency to her unpacking and organizing of the birth supplies. But with me, she is all calm and positivity. "You're doing beautifully, Shannon! Just amazing. You're going to meet your baby in no time." I don't believe her. I've told that same lie to plenty of women. *We have hours ahead of us,* I tell myself.

Renee's presence is the opposite of intrusive, and despite not believing her time estimate, I implicitly trust her. The minute she walks in the door, though I can't express it, I welcome her into this experience. She is a known and trustworthy presence in my home, one who has demonstrated her care for me and my baby since the embryonic stage. Another sociologist, Barbara Katz Rothman, describes the mutually beneficial relationship between midwife and mother: "To trust the home as a place for birth is to fundamentally trust the woman to know how to give birth and the midwife to know how to help her." If Renee is home with me, it's because the baby and I are safe here. Knowing this I can surrender to the contractions that are now relentless in their arrival.

Needing to put my pain-relief plan into action I ask, "Renee, can I get in the tub?"

Once it's been filled with a garden hose connected to the kitchen faucet, I slowly sink into the warm, alleviating water of the birth tub, dubbed the "midwife's epidural" for the muscular relaxation it provides. The water eases my shoulders away from my ears and causes a deeper letting go of my muscles than the chants and vibrations of my vocalizing can. After just a few more contractions in the tub, the sensations suddenly change; there is a bowling ball taking up space where my baby should be. I'm about to explain this to Renee when the next wave hits, but instead of chanting "Open," I cannot help but to bear down against this hard, round thing in my pelvis.

"Good job, Shannon! Just like that, go with your body and push," offers Renee.

Push?! I'm already pushing?! I don't want to believe it. I'm holding back because I think it's going to get so much worse, but this is it? I'm confused and need Najeeb to ground me. He holds my hand and whispers in my ear everything I need to hear. *You can do this. We're going to meet our baby soon.*

Now with each contraction I am involuntarily pushing with the pressure, and I hate it. I cannot surrender each muscle as I had been doing; I need to engage new muscles I never knew I had. It is a masculine energy I had not been expecting labor to require, all outward and flexed. The upper segment of my uterus is no longer pulling the turtleneck over my baby's head; it is now pushing it through the opening. Renee shines a flashlight into the water, "I can see the top of baby's head. Keep going!" That makes no sense to me—there is no way to *not* keep going, my body requiring me to push whether I like it or not. I shake with the effort.

There is a burning sensation. Perineal muscles are stretching around the pressure, and I start to believe that that hard round ball is a baby, and that it's going to split me into halves. "Allah!" I cry out. One more push, and the pressure is gone, the contractions cease. Like a fish coming up for air, my baby's body careens to the surface.

"I love you! I love you! I love you sooooo much!" are the first words my baby hears, and my first truth as a mother; without anything received or bartered, with no conditions or even self-consciousness—it is ecstasy in the true meaning of the word, *to stand outside oneself*—and my spirit immediately and forever loves this being. This love is a command, a metaphysical truth about the result of difficulties and trials. *With every difficulty there is ease,* an oft-quoted verse from the Qur'an, immediately imprints on my every cell, the armor of cynicism the modern world asks of us sloughed off in light of the miraculous.

I gaze at my baby's face as he does a back float in the water, his wide brown eyes searching the room; he looks like my Uncle Pat and my brother Shawn. He is as familiar to me as the moles on my arms. Of course, it's a boy. I have known you. It's Salek—spiritual voyager—we have traveled together, my organs shifting for you, my food siphoned off to sustain your rapid growth, and now my spirit, upon seeing yours, reaching a new, heretofore unimagined height, motherhood. It feels like the pinnacle of womanly achievement.

The British obstetrician Grantly Dick Read, in his classic book, *Childbirth Without Fear*, writes of this very moment:

> [I have been so] profoundly impressed by the inexplicable transfiguration of women at the moment of their baby's birth, that I have been led, as usual, to ask: why this? It is not sentimentality; it is not relief from suffering; it is not simply satisfaction of accomplishment. It is bigger than

all of those things. Can it be the Creator intended to draw mothers nearest to Himself at the moment of love's fulfillment?

I have studied the waxing cervix and the subsequent push of one human out of another human; these are acts of birth, acts that modern obstetrics obsesses over. What they neglect and what DeLee's students must have observed in birth outside of the hospital is this crowning and glorious moment between a mother and her son, a mother and her Creator, yet our culture only wants to make "real" the mechanics of birth. As C. S. Lewis describes mechanistic biology, "Thus in birth the blood and pain are real, the rejoicing a mere subjective point of view." As if the birth of a human is simply the cracking of a shell after having been warmed a requisite number of days, the shell composted and forgotten. To fully participate, without medications or the gaze of strangers, to feel every contraction and the endorphin surge in response, to love deeper than you ever knew possible, to be a vehicle in God's soaring act of the birth of His creation— these are the open doors and secrets of women and the midwives who watch over them. This is what hospitals scoff at.

But now I know that birth is more than the hours of dilation leading up to this moment in the kiddie pool, more than learning to soften through the contractions, more than pushing into the pressure. Birth is created for this ecstatic moment. It's as real as the downy hair on Salek's head and the turn of his face toward my voice, "I love you Salek."

The perfection of human love is a mother, moments after birth.

# CHAPTER 4

*Hide yourselves, you who search for knowledge, this will save*
*you from trials and sorrows,*
*Have determination, thus you will surpass your generation.*
*Do not grieve for the trials which come upon you,*
*Be courageous, so that people believe you want for nothing.*
*For the Science is never granted to one who fears hunger,*
*God raises his servant who shows patience.*

—Shaykh Amadou Bamba

Hadigay, her name the West African form of Khadija, the Prophet's first wife, stands to my right; Sandra, the midwife from New Mexico, to my left. In front of us lies a woman, legs in stirrups, whom I have just finished suturing under Sandra and Hadigay's supervision. Or so I thought.

Hadigay, a stout and choleric Senegalese midwife, is unhappy with how we have left the suturing job. In rough French, she tells Sandra that my suturing hasn't gone far enough. Sandra, who came of age as a midwife during the seventies, refuses to go beyond what she perceives is the anatomically correct repair I have just performed.

The "husband's knot," rarely tied in the West and likewise performed in only the most rural regions of Senegal, is a procedure in which more stitches than are anatomically appropriate keep a woman's vaginal opening taut after the grand stretching it has just undergone in the birthing process. In the 1970s, many American women, once oblivious that the procedure had been done to them, revolted against it, casting it as a misogynistic practice that deformed the bodies of women for the pleasure of men, often leaving women with a lifetime of unnecessary pain and discomfort.

Hadigay insists that I tie the husband's knot on the patient lying before us. While my gut does not want to add the extra stitch, I am uncertain how to refute Hadigay, who is both my elder and my sister in Islam.

 

Dakar, once the center of the transatlantic slave trade, now the capital of Senegal, is somnolent when we arrive. Only a few women are out sweeping their front stoops, the heat already forming in the air above their heads, their sweeps slowed by its gravity. Najeeb and I heave Salek along with our luggage toward the group of white women with Birkenstocks, some of whom are already accessorizing with African fabrics. We have all come as a part of the African Birth Collective, a misleading name as it's an American midwife who will supervise and teach us midwifery students, while we deliver the babies of West African mothers. In exchange for the experience, the clinics in rural Senegal are supplied with much-needed American donations and equipment. Our group alone has collected enough funds for a vehicle that will serve as the clinic's ambulance.

We acquaint ourselves with one another as we walk in the otherwise empty airport parking lot to the van that waits to take us three hours to Mboro, the coastal town where the birthing clinic resides. Most of the midwifery students are from the West Coast—Portland, San Francisco, Los Angeles—and most are childless, single women. I immediately take a liking to Sandra, the midwife who will be signing off and supervising our clinical work. She has the telltale skin of winters spent in the dry climate of New Mexico: tanned, and softly lined around the eyes.

As we walk she plays peekaboo with Salek and tells me, "I've always practiced midwifery care at the stage of life I'm in. When I was younger and in my childbearing days, I delivered babies at home. When my kids got older and needed me more, I moved to an office setting with scheduled hours and did well-woman care. Now I'm in menopause, and I work as a midwife in an office that offers bio-identical hormones to menopausal women."

Her sensible approach to midwifery with a family appealed to my pragmatism, and vice versa. She later confided in me that she was concerned that most of these natural-minded students had opted out of taking chloroquine to prevent malaria, her time as a Peace Corps volunteer in Mali informing her fears of the disease. She's relieved when I tell her we are taking antimalarials, even if it was a capsule of *artemsia annua*, a Chinese herb recommended by our acupuncturist. She seemed to respect that we didn't possess a knee-jerk rejection of medication.

In Senegal, vans, and nearly everything else, including boats and water jugs, are highly decorated. *Alhamdoulilahi*—"All praise to Allah"—is inscribed on the hood of our van, and the colors of the Senegalese flag—red, yellow, and green—splash across the rest of the van's body. Our driver, dreadlocked with dhikr beads encircled around his neck, opens the doors for us. "Welcome to Africa! I am Ahmad," he beams, ushering everyone inside onto the peeling benches.

When he sees my husband's beard and my long skirt and hijab, he cries in surprise, "Salam alaykum!" He grabs my husband's hand and pulls him in for a bro hug, tousles Salek's hair, and puts his hand over his heart and bows slightly in a greeting to me. The other American students gape: Did we know this driver? Why was his greeting to us so much more enthusiastic? We feel right at home and take a seat.

Ahmad stows our luggage on the roof of the van, and we are ready to go. Except, we aren't. Turning the key, the van chugs and sputters but refuses to start. Again and again, Ahmad turns the key, and it teases a start, but then nothing. A crowd of men gathers around the hood of the car, inspecting the engine as Ahmad continues to turn the key. Their findings reveal zero, the car will not move. The tallest of the bunch slams down the hood, forfeiting a material explanation; he holds up his hands, palms turned skyward seeking a spiritual solution. The other men follow suit, as does our driver Ahmad. They're supplicating. In a booming African voice, the tallest man rings out a prayer in Wolof, the most widely spoken language in Senegal. The men around him, skin glistening in the rising morning sun, chorus, "Amin ya Rabb. Amin, ya Rabb."

Ahmad then resettles behind the steering wheel, turns the ignition, and this time, it starts. The other students don't understand what just occurred—our journey up the coast of Africa is fueled by answered prayers.

℘

The Mboro maternity clinic is similar in degree to what we would call a birth center in the United States; there are rooms for women to labor, there are midwives to attend them, and there is no immediate access to an operating room. It differs, however, in kind. Void of jacuzzi tubs, essential oil diffusers, organic sheets, and a birthing ball, the laboring room consists of three vinyl-covered narrow beds where the women labor communally until birth is imminent, when they're moved to the delivery room, taking one of two narrow exam tables. At the back of the clinic, there is a large postpartum room with windows built close to the ceiling to ensure privacy. The room feels like a celebration; the women remove their colorful turbans and hijabs and enjoy a good rest as relatives deliver food for seven days. The waiting room is an outdoor, open-air plaza, lined with benches and a sunshade, where families can often be seen spreading a woven plastic mat, uncovering plates of grilled tomatoes, fish, millet, and a local mashed yam, rolled into a small ball, and plopped into your mouth like popcorn. If you are lucky enough to be outside on your break for one of these feasts, they will insist you fill your belly, and that you do it before anyone else.

During one of my first shifts in the clinic, Sandra and I evaluate a girl who can't be more than sixteen, her bright pink turban tied in a bow on top of her head, framing a face that hasn't yet lost its baby fat. Her easy smile belies the fact that she has been having contractions for days. Sandra speaks fluent French, although in the more rural areas where we are, not everyone has been educated in the French schools. Most speak only Wolof. Luckily, birth speak is rudimentary in any language. Sandra asks the girl a few questions, but it becomes apparent that after days of labor, any French she acquired has receded to unreachable portions of her brain. She motions to us to open the door.

We follow her command and are surprised to see a man in the hallway—in this Muslim country, men do not enter women's spaces, particularly in health care settings—acting like the proverbial nervous father, wringing his hands and pacing. But we are confused. Is this her father? He's old enough to be her grandfather, his grey beard framing a deeply lined face, a tattered turban barely concealing a bald head. He self-consciously tells us, the two American women, that this is his wife, his fourth wife, and that she has been in labor for three days. Their village midwife, uncomfortable with the lack of progress, told them to make the journey to our clinic.

After a cervical exam that reveals a narrow pelvis and a swollen cervix, Sandra fumes aloud in English, so he can't understand, "I doubt she's even sixteen! Her pelvis is not even properly developed yet, add onto that the malnutrition here, and this is a textbook obstructed labor. Fourth wife! How many wives does he need? Why take such a young one?! We have nothing for her here. She needs an epidural, Pitocin, and most likely, a Cesarean section or the baby, or she, could die." I look at the laboring mother swaying to yet another contraction, her belly protruding beneath her shirt.

In the United States, the most common reason for transfer to the hospital from a planned home birth is failure to progress, a non-emergency. *Failure to progress* is an imprecise term defined differently from provider to provider, with some obstetricians conservatively measuring progress as cervical dilation of one centimeter per hour. Midwives tend to individualize their assessments, and if mother and baby are clinically well—hydrated, no fevers, nourished, fetal heart rate steady and responsive—then the labor can unfold at its own pace. Even with this more liberal approach, labors can stall and sputter, leaving the mother and baby at risk of exhaustion and possibly infection. If this labor were happening at a birth center or a home back in the States, the remedy would be to call up the local labor and delivery unit and inform them that we are bringing in a mother who is failing to progress and who needs therapeutic rest in the form of an epidural and an augmentation of her labor with Pitocin. Then with great disappointment, we pack up our birth kits and head to the hospital, usually no more than a fifteen-minute commute.

However, in labors like this teenager's, labors that have gone on for days and are likely not only failing to progress but also complicated by an obstruction, a surgical solution is required. Obstruction of labor occurs when the baby's presenting part is not advancing despite, in this case, days of strong contractions. Usually, either the baby is too large in relation to the pelvis or the mother's pelvis is constricted or both. Malnutrition, having a baby before the pelvis is fully developed, and lack of access to surgical care combine to make these harrowing labors more common in less developed parts of the world.

Due to her obstructed labor, this young woman is at risk of developing an obstetric fistula, a hole created by the constant pressure exerted by the baby on the mother's pelvic musculature, reducing blood flow to the surrounding tissues, eventually causing them to necrotize and form a permanent hole between the vagina and the bladder or the vagina and the rectum, depending on the baby's position. This hole, or fistula, leaves the woman without muscles to hold her urine or feces, resulting in an ever-present drip of these fluids, causing a lifetime of shame, infections, and, in some extreme cases, abandonment by her family and community.

As soon as a contraction ends, the corners of the young mother's mouth turn up shyly, unaware that even we Americans are helpless to execute a U-turn in her labor. The father pleads to keep her here in the clinic, as it is very expensive to hire a driver to take his wife to the nearest hospital in Thies, a forty-eight-kilometer ride away. Once there, we are told, he will have to pay in advance for any medical procedures suggested by the hospital staff. He looks defeated as we convey the urgency of his wife's situation.

Sandra just looks pissed.

In this moment, though, he is a father, deeply concerned about the well-being of his wife and child—so concerned, in fact, that he has breached his own cultural and religious norms of conduct to enter the all-female maternity ward. I help his wife outside. He gives *salaams* to me as we pack her in the makeshift ambulance——an old station wagon with the middle seats removed—provided by the donations of American women who would never know the desperation of such a situation

ᏸᎧ

We don't have long to ponder her fate, as the next woman is quickly brought into the delivery room. The Senegalese midwives attend each delivery alongside the Americans, often acting as translators and sometimes as enforcers of a birth culture that American midwifery students often buck. It's an old story— thinking they are "helping," the students insist on getting mothers up and moving during labor, while the Senegalese women prefer to lie down and rest, even during a contraction, something midwives in the States discourage.

The new arrival closes her eyes to shut out the students asking her to sit up, her hair a halo of frizz about her small face. She shows no signs of need, signaling to everyone that she's got this. I look out the window to give her some privacy. There are goats wandering around the clinic's yard, their bells and bleats tinkling in our ears. If I know anything about birth at this point in my training, it's that most mammals, including women, do not like to be observed as they labor.

"Ya Latif!!!! Ya Latif! Ya Latif. Ya Latiiiiiiif!" she cries out as the next contraction hits, swatting away the midwives still attempting to move her. I spin around and my heart leaps. I understand her. Latif is a name of God, one of many that Muslims call upon to express a specific divine virtue. Latif, the Gentle One. What a perfect antidote to the ferocity of contractions. She is calling on Allah's gentle qualities, His ability to know the subtleties of things. Our eyes connect, and I nod softly.

She resettles onto the bare delivery table, a vinyl table without even a cover—the table, along with the gloves used for the deliveries, are disinfected with bleach between births. Nothing is wasted here; the women use their old skirts as pads to absorb the postpartum bleeding. On her back, and pushing with all her might, she is still muttering "Ya Latif" as the next contraction winds down. I brush her hair back, wishing for a cold washcloth to wipe the sweat from her brow, to cool the back of her neck, but even that is a luxury. I think of the births back home, where a cold washcloth isn't enough for moms, where we walk to the freezer with a bowl, pile up cubes of ice, add water, and frequently refresh the washcloth so that it feels as if we have dipped it into waters of the Arctic.

"Shannon, if you want to catch the baby, now is the time to glove up!" Sandra says while peering at the vaginal outlet. "I see hair!"

"Okay. If I can make it!"

Another contraction begins to the refrain of "Ya Latif," and my hand is subsequently squeezed. *Ya Latif, be gentle with my hand!* Once she lets go, I run to put gloves on and sit on the stool between her legs, where I see tightly curled hair peeking out. Sandra shows me how to support the baby's head and the mother's perineum in order to prevent any tearing and the subsequent need to suture.

"Usually, we would use oil, or hot compresses now," Sandra instructs. "But since we have none of that available, I want you to focus on keeping the baby's head flexed with one hand and offering gentle perineal support with the other." I'm trying to follow her instructions, when suddenly the baby blasts into my hands, in a bath of amniotic fluid and blood—the baby's decisive cries announce his arrival. The mother puts her hand across her forehead and leans back without even looking at the baby. Her work is done, and she needs a minute. Again, I notice the American midwifery students obliviously encourage their cultural norms of emotional expressiveness onto the more private and reserved Senegalese by immediately wanting to put the baby on his mother's chest for skin-to-skin contact and bonding.

The clinic's Senegalese midwives, keen to this faux pas, rush to the mother and cut the cord, whisking the baby away to the counter, where they clean him. He's wrapped in the flannel blankets and topped with a knit newborn hat that the Americans brought, a coveted item in the clinic. When all that's done, they bring the baby to me rather than to the mother, as if I pushed him out myself! I look to see if the mother is ready to be presented with her baby. She smiles wanly at me, spent but happy.

I point to the bonny boy and tell her, "Abdul Latif." Servant of the Gentle One, a common name in the Muslim world.

"Abdul Latif. Oui. Merci. Thank you." She smiles, and her whole being illumines as she reaches for her baby.

&#8365;&#8359;

On my days off, we walk the nearby coastline to watch the wooden fishing boats, painted in Senegalese fashion, red, yellow, green, *Alhamdoulellah, bismillah* written in Latin and Arabic fonts. At dawn, I hear the call to prayer, given without a microphone or speaker, the muezzin's natural voice rousing me better than any alarm clock. Along with the cooks and the patriarch of the compound we are staying at, we make *wudu* outside in the cool morning air, taking turns using what looks like a plastic tea kettle. In the hot afternoons, we take a cab, really just a car that goes back and forth the three kilometers between our compound and the main streets of Mboro. There, a ruby-red, sweetened hibiscus tea is sold in plastic bags; drinking it necessitates biting off the corner and squirting the sugary liquid straight into your parched mouth. Nothing quenches a hot African afternoon better than this sweetened tea reminiscent of Kool Aid. Yogurt is also sold in plastic bags, the vat it ferments in as large as a back-yard kiddie pool. Salek, now nine months old and experiment-ing with food, loves both treats, so we frequently make stops at the stalls.

Salek's full name is Muhammad Salek, but we normally call him by his middle name. Here in Senegal, though, when people ask us his name, we say Muhammad because it is more common and, because of its namesake, beloved. Salek is invariably met with a hearty *"Muhammad!,"* a kiss, and a hair tousle. This is our way into Senegalese generosity; we receive socks, fruit, and even, from one tailor, an entire traditional Senegalese outfit! One evening, we are in town and stay to pray *maghrib* at the mosque. As the prayers were finishing, we noticed the crowd walking down the street, and we hear a communal recitation.

"Muhammad! Muhammad!" calls someone who had met us before the prayer. "You come, you come with me." He grabs my husband by the hand and leads us into a jam-packed room, men in the front and women in the back. The men are singing songs praising Allah and His Messenger—they clap and throw their heads back, their teeth straight and strong, as they belt out the chorus, "La ilaha illa Allah. La ilaha illa Allah. Muhammadun Rasul Allah. La ilaha illa Allah."

In the back the women stand, old women who needed the help of younger relatives to rise, young women curvy and buxom, all swaying and raising their hands to the rhythms of the chants. The Senegalese are embodied people; they take up all of the space they inhabit in their physical form with an ease and

68

grace I had rarely seen in America. Middle-aged women do not try to hide their figures; they let it add to their gravitas, lending indisputable authority—queens. Now, that embodiment let loose; everyone moving to their own rhythm—there is no line dancing, no need to conform to the beat, to each her joyful own.

There exist many theories that while Mississippi is the birthplace of the blues, this West African soil, on which I am delivering babies and singing praise poetry, is home to some of their deepest roots. Sylviane Diouf, a social historian, has written on Islam's connection to the blues: "Several elements from West and Central Africa, Islamic and not, went into the creation of the blues and its predecessor, the holler, including Sufi chanting and the call to prayer. And the tradition of *du'a* or supplication fits right into this melodic and spiritual frame." The blues of *du'a*.

"La ilaha illa Allah. La ilaha illa Allah. Muhammadun Rasul Allah. La ilaha illa Allah." I am singing the chorus, standing and clapping, timidly finding my feet beneath me. The harmonies are familiar, the wistful way the solo singer sings, reminiscent of a childhood soundtrack—the blues.

Sunday mornings after Mass, my dad took us to church.

In the car, barely out of the church parking lot, he would turn the dial to find the Sunday morning blues hour on the local Minneapolis radio station. The small speakers rattled from the doors in the backseat. As the singer's plaintive voice rang out, it resonated with my longing for a complete family.

"Shannon, do you know how you can tell if it's the blues?" my father would shout over the music. He was lighter, more relaxed and self-assured than moments earlier, when genuflecting and reciting by rote the Catholic Creed.

"No, how?" My father, a divorced single parent and a veteran of Vietnam, also placed his loss at the feet of the blues. An entire spice route split our losses into unequal halves, but when the blues played, the distance of our pain shrunk to the space between the tan-upholstered front seat and the back seat. In that shared listening I found a forgiveness—the sharp edges of our losses finding reprieve together.

"If you can clap your hands or stomp your feet to it, it's the blues," he would say, turning the volume dial up and slapping the steering wheel.

*La ilaha illa Allah Muhammad Rasul Allah.* My feet stomp the dirt floor, I clap my hands, and a longing bubbles up in me, not the old longing for family—those are the blues of a different order—but the longing for the divine. As we sing the chorus I feel a deep belonging. *La ilaha illa Allah Muhammad Rasul Allah.*

My hands clap, my feet stomp. It must be the blues.

℘

Hadigay grabs my arm and moves it to the woman's perineum. "One more," she tells me. Sandra is on the other side, telling me to put down the needle holder and step away, which I do.

Hadigay then grabs me by the shoulders and works our connection.

Pointing to herself, she tells me, "Hajja! I am Hajja Hadigay. One more!" She moves my hand to pick up the instrument.

She is telling me that she has made the pilgrimage to Mecca—Hajja being an honorific title given to those who return home from the pilgrimage. It is a title that demands respect.

Meanwhile, Sandra is talking sternly into my ear: "Do not tie one more suture. It will leave her in pain and cause her uncomfortable sex for the rest of her life."

When I refuse to pick up the instrument, Hadigay, clearly frustrated by my lack of manners, takes a step toward me and says admonishingly, "Astaghfirullah!" and then storms from the room.

My two worlds are tied up like the knot that I ultimately leave untied at this woman's perineum. I'm left with a familiar sense of not meeting the mark on either side of the fence.

൫

We have one more stop before leaving Senegal. Islam, like Catholicism, is a faith that believes in saints, people whose souls ascend so near to God that the Arabic word for "saints," *wali*, means "friend of God."

It is widely agreed upon that one of those friends is the Senegalese scholar Shaykh Ahmadou Bamba. In 1895, the colonizing French government arrested Shaykh Bamba on the false premise that he and his followers were planning a revolt against the French. Sometimes called the African Gandhi, Shaykh Bamba rejected violence as a means to overthrow the colonizers.

Stories of his miracles are numerous. Once, after he was arrested and sent into exile on a ship bound for Gabon, a country along the Atlantic coast of Africa, the time for afternoon prayer was nearly gone. Shaykh Bamba asked the French crew repeatedly for an opportunity to pray but was denied each time. With minutes to spare, he disembarked from the boat, stepping on a prayer rug floating on the water. He prayed his afternoon prayer on the sea, then got back on the boat.

Along pockmarked, and in many places unpaved, roads, our little family of three heads east into the heartland of Senegal to the city of Touba, where Shaykh Ahmadou Bamba is buried. Our driver knows the way despite the lack of signage.

When we arrive, a familiar energy greets us—it is what brought us on this pilgrimage to Touba: *baraka*. I recognize it as the same energy that I have encountered while sitting at the feet of teachers back at Zaytuna, visiting the Prophet Muhammad ﷺ in Medina, and kneeling beside birthing mothers. *Baraka* is an Arabic word commonly translated as "blessing." It's an unadulterated source of spiritual potency and can be concentrated in people, especially pious ones, or places, like Mecca or Jerusalem, or even in objects used by a righteous person. In Senegal, they believe that *baraka* is often concentrated in mothers.

After stopping for lunch, an unforgettable goat stew with a peanut tomato sauce, we arrive at one of the largest mosques in

Africa, the Great Mosque of Touba. Domes of bright blue and green brighten the soft gray exterior, and a minaret towers above us at 250 feet high. The marble floors cool my feet, and the yellow and blue stained glass hexagon windows, my eyes. Men in their *boubas*—three-piece outfits consisting of trousers, a tunic, and a flowing colorful piece of fabric draped over the top—slide gigantic prayer beads between their fingers. Women bent over the Qur'an stand, reciting softly as they wait for the next prayer's *adhan*. No one acts surprised to see us. In the presence of spiritual greats, destiny is its own logic: we are here, so we must know.

We enter the room with the tomb. A low gate surrounds it with cushions for supplicants to settle on. I kneel down and cup my palms, my throat a folding file of prayers—*Through the presence of this blessed man, O God, hear and answer my supplications.* I was a soul beseeching her Lord at the feet of someone who had gotten further along the path than I. Prayers spilled forth in an almost rhythmic incantation. The home of the blues indeed.

Many of those prayers would go on to be answered in ways and means I could never, and still can hardly, fathom. Latif, the name of Allah that the mother back in the delivery room beseeched, the name that encompasses His gentleness and His ability to know the subtle nature of everything, the hardness of the beak needed by a chick to break the shell, the jelly needed in the umbilical cord to protect the arteries and vein encased within, the need for Shannon to travel to the tomb of a West African saint to facilitate her growth as a midwife, as a Muslim, as a human. *Ya Latif, thank you for the many kind and subtle ways in which you nurture me.*

And so upturned palms and answered prayers had ushered us into Africa, and now upturned palms and answered prayers usher us out of Africa too.

# CHAPTER 5

*Out beyond ideas of wrongdoing and rightdoing, there is a
field. I'll meet you there.*

—Rumi, as interpreted by Coleman Barks

It's 2:25 in the morning, and every three minutes, a moan
reaches our ears from the birth center's womblike and win-
dowless Pink Room. Around a table, littered with Noah's Bagels
wrappers, sesame seeds, and smears of cream cheese, huddle two
tired midwifery students and their raconteur, Judy, who, as
usual, is mid-story.

"So, then, even though the baby was posterior and asynclitic,
I was able to put my finger on its anterior fontanelle and rotate
its little head, like an old rotary phone, into an anterior position.
Then, wow, she really felt like pushing! Her mother was suppos-
edly a childbirth educator herself, but all she did was wring her
hands and make a sour puss face in the corner, and I tell you,
what a nut job! Anyhow, I move the woman to a side lying position…" She takes a sip of her diet soda, raises her eyebrows,
perfectly shaded, even at this hour, in an ombré of chartreuse. A
divorced mother of three with a bleached blond pixie cut, a pen-
chant for gel nail extensions, and a generous heart, Judy has sunk
her life savings into Sage Femme Birth Center with a real commitment to serving women of all classes, rare in the San

Francisco Bay Area, where midwifery often functions as a boutique service.

As she attempts to continue her tale, the moans turn into grunts, interrupting us and signaling that the mother in the Pink Room is ready to push. I often feel like I'm in a version of One Thousand and One Nights, held captive by Judy's stories, almost always interrupted by the penetrating sounds of a woman in labor, so that we never quite get to the end of one, only to begin the next night's story with a new set of characters.

Sage Femme is nestled on a side street off the 16th St. Mission BART station in San Francisco's colorful Mission District, still a real Latino neighborhood full of flair, paint-saturated murals, burrito shops, and street vendors selling mangos dusted with chili powder. In its dark and damp corners, the Mission is also an open-air drug market. After one of the first births I had attended at Sage Femme, following an early-morning witness to the miraculous entrance of room air into fresh lungs, the parents still tucked up in their birth room, I encountered a man blocking the doorway, curled into the same fetal position this newborn had gestated in, slowly advancing a needle into his arm, preventing my exit. The stark contrast of seeing someone dull the gift of consciousness I had just witnessed emerging was so jarring that I hesitated to return.

&

Tuesday and Thursday mornings, I take the BART train beneath the waters of the bay, reciting a litany, a *wird* in Arabic, as I travel. A *wird*, which literally means "a place of water," consists of verses from the Qur'an and prophetic supplications. There are many reasons to recite a litany in the morning and evening— protection, comfort, delight—but encountering the hustle and bustle of morning commuters who exit at Embarcadero to the addicts I weave through at my 16th St. Mission stop, carefully holding my skirt above the urine-stained concrete as I walk north to Capp Street, I find the recitation as necessary as the water bottle I diligently carry with me. Remembering God in the midst of urban America is like drinking a tall glass of water.

Over the years my community has homogenized. Outside of my BART trips to the birth center, my social circle has become a bubble of devout Muslim seekers. Arabic peppers my everyday speech; there is never a plan made that isn't followed up with an *insha'Allah*; a baby's cuteness remarked upon immediately prompts a *masha'Allah* so as not to garner the evil eye. The only pants I own are yoga pants, worn to births or changed into at home; long skirts, tunics and hijabs are the cultural currency I barter when with the Muslims and the loss on investment I weather when not.

Muslims are not the Amish, averse to culture or technological advancements; in fact for most of Islam's history, traditions of Muslim knowledge have emerged from major urban areas, such as Cairo, Cordoba, and Baghdad. But in twenty-first-century urban America, with its liberated sexual norms, deteriorating family values, and consumer excesses, committed Muslims, like moths, gravitate from the darkness they perceive toward the light, finding repose in the company of like-minded seekers. For some, though, it is the darkness from which they flee that defines their connection, not the light to which they are drawn.

Walking down the long hallway into the cool, subterranean, cavernous birth center, the office manager, Christina, hands me my schedule for the day. I notice that at one o'clock, I have an initial visit with a woman named Sadie.

"Shannon," says Judy, walking into the office, already abuzz with the day's energy, "today you're going to see Sadie. I spoke with her on the phone. She is pregnant via IVF. Her partner, Jeff, is transgender, and they used his brother's sperm to make the baby."

My brain cannot comprehend the relationship between the verbs and the pronouns in this patient report. The Arabic from the *wird* I just recited is playing a loop in my head, as if it is all the answer I need. *Bismallahi'lladhi la yadurru ma 'asmihi shay'un fi'l-ardi wa la fi sama'i, wa huwa's Sami'u'l Alim.* In the name of Allah, with Whose Name nothing on earth or in heaven can harm. He is the Hearer, the Knower.

The fluid natures of the pronouns have me stumped. This is still in the early aughts, well before transgenderism became a cultural flashpoint. What does it mean, "he"? Is he a he now, or was he a he before? And is Sadie really a Sadie? Sperm from the brother has contributed to the baby Sadie is carrying, so this makes the baby the nephew of the dad?

"Oh, and Sadie is a convert to Judaism, so I thought you two would have a lot in common!" says Judy, the epitome of an open-minded San Franciscan, before taking a stack of charts and walking out of the front office. I haven't even set my things down, yet it feels as if decades have passed, and I'm in a future when rules of grammar, basic means of human conception, and religious norms are profoundly altered.

By lunchtime I can hardly enjoy my usual nachos supreme that Christina brings me, the chips going soggy and limp under the weight of the crema. I'm thinking about gender. Motherhood, along with being a Muslim woman, has in many ways solidified my conceptions of gender. When a man unrelated to me is in the room—my sister's boyfriend, for example—I cover my hair per the Qur'anic prescription. I celebrate the feminine function and form in my work. I love being a woman. How can someone deny the power and beauty embedded in women? Why would someone reject this to become a *him*? Islam reinforces women's unique roles in society, as well as in the home. Midwifery reclaims that understanding of the hidden miracles and wonders that God encases in our own unique anatomy.

Aisha, the beloved, brilliant, red-haired wife of the Prophet, relates that the Prophet ﷺ said, "The word 'womb' derives its name from 'The Merciful.' So whoever keeps good relations with it, God will keep good relations with him, and whosoever will sever it, God too will sever His relations with him."

It was hard not to place Jeff in the latter category. Finishing my nachos, I circumscribe the gender lines as I understand them and steel myself for the upcoming prenatal.

&#8352;

One o'clock arrives, and Sadie blows in like the breeze off the bay, cool and relentless. Petite and curvy, she's wearing a leopard-print bodycon dress that barely squeezes over her burgeoning belly, a vintage clutch, rainbow-print leggings, large round sunglasses, and flip-flops. When she smiles at me, the gap between her front two teeth highlights her adorable heart-shaped face and suits her colorful persona.

She surprises me with an immediate hug. "I'm Sadie. You must be Shannon. Judy told me you would be my student. My partner is parking the car. He'll be right in."

*He'll.* I have taken an immediate liking to her, yet when she says *he'll*, I'm reminded of the situation. *Bismillah,* I think, *let's just get this over with.* I lead her to the modern rust-colored sectionals where we conduct the first part of our prenatal visits. I fetch her chart and spy her partner walking past the office. Although petite, he, for all practical purposes, is really a he; there's the scruffy beginnings of a beard, a baseball cap, saggy jeans, and a ringer t-shirt.

"Cheers, Shannon!" he shakes my hand. "I'm Jeff, Sadie's partner." His South African accent catches me off guard and charms me all at once. I muster a smile and quickly retreat to the couch where Sadie is waiting for us.

"It's so nice to meet both of you. Welcome! Today we are going to go through your medical history and talk a little about how this pregnancy has been going for you so far. Judy has told me a little about your, uh, your situation. I mean pregnancy! She's told me about your pregnancy, or, uh, how you got pregnant." I stutter and blush. This is not going well.

Thank God for Sadie's exuberance. "Yes! We got pregnant on the first IVF cycle. It was a miracle! We used Jeff's brother's sperm so that the baby could be a part of both of us. I had so much morning sickness, it was the worst. Now that's all behind me, and I have sciatica and cankles. That's my pregnancy!"

We laugh and wrap up the intake portion of the visit. Moving to the exam room, Sadie waddles up onto the exam table. I grab the measuring tape and Doppler as she lifts her tight dress, with some difficulty, above her belly.

First, I check her baby's position. Facing her feet, I feel between her iliac crests for the head by pushing my two hands toward each other. If there is a nice round, ballottable mass between them, it's a head. I then trace with my fingertips up one side or the other, feeling for the continuous curve of the back, until I reach the large lump of rump and knees. If I feel lots of limbs, the baby is posterior, its back touching mother's back; if not, it's anterior, a more ideal position for baby during the labor process. Sadie's baby is posterior.

Jeff comes around to feel what I feel, and I show him the ideal spot to feel the kicks. He leans down close to baby's head and whispers, "Hello, little one. We can't wait to meet you. Thank you for coming to us." I measure the baby and apply the Doppler and, as the healthy heartbeat bumpity-bumps, I think, *Jeff must be jealous, or at least sad, that he has sacrificed the ability to experience this within him*, but when I look up there are joy-filled tears glistening in his eyes.

๛

I begin looking forward to my Thursday appointments with Sadie. I ask her about converting to Judaism, Jeff's faith. From her I learn about Shabbat, how she looks forward to the candle-light and community on the Sabbath, and how Judaism has given her a sense of the sacred, which she had been lacking. We laugh as she tells me she is looking forward to settling into the stereotypical Jewish mother role.

Jeff I'm not so sure about. My hijab seems quaint and old-fashioned next to the beard and ace bandages wrapping his boobs—a quill dipped in black ink beside a sleek, cold laptop. Although there are similarities between us two women existing in different communities than the one they were born into, our two paths were in fact entirely different. Islam offered me a framework to see myself in relation to God, to live life in a way that aligned me to the Creator's wish for His creation—to know Him. He had fashioned the veins on the leaves and molded the clay of my physical form as well, and to Him I would return; thus I owed a debt of gratitude and worship. I chose a well-trodden path, and to follow it, I need only to fix my feet in the footprints of those who have gone before.

Jeff's path, on the other hand, seems his alone, a life charted purely by his innermost convictions, his alone to discover and actualize, he, the potter and the wheel.

What if our choices are a reaction against the same thing? Is this our way of saying no to the flattening forces of modern America? The thought unnerves me, and I turn back to the burgeoning mother in front of me.

ℰℭ

One week after her due date, flip-flops are now a must for Sadie, the swelling in her feet making any other shoe impossible. Sadie lumbers up onto the exam table. I take her blood pressure, and it's high.

"Hmmmm," I say. "Your blood pressure is up. Maybe you're stressed about going over your due date. Let's take it one more time after we check the baby." We do, and it's still high. I order some labs to rule out preeclampsia, including a 24-hour urine test to gauge whether or not the kidneys are spilling protein into the urine, a sign of severe preeclampsia. I hand her the outsize plastic container, a gallon of milk redux.

"Oh great, now I have to piss in here for the next 24 hours. I really can't wait for this to be over. Do you think it's preeclampsia, Shannon? I don't want to go to the hospital!"

The next day, when her protein levels return elevated, we abort any plans for an out-of-hospital birth. This pregnancy must come to an end in a hospital for the safety of mother and baby.

I call Judy to update her. Judy is an encyclopedia of obstetrics. She knows every facet of pregnancy complications, preventative measures to avoid said complications, variations of normal birth, breastfeeding issues, and the resources to help with that. When she encountered one of these problems, like a puppy wrangling a chew toy, Judy would not give up until it was resolved. Conversations on the phone with her spanned hours, during which my two-year-old zoned out on *Thomas the Train* episodes, while she droned on about the grams of protein needed to prevent preeclampsia or the latest study on moxibustion to turn a breech baby; each call was a crash course in midwifery.

"Well, I'm not surprised. IVF mothers have an increased chance of developing preeclampsia. That chance increases even more when the sperm is from a donor." I sit down for what I know will be an extended lesson. "Over time a mother's body develops a tolerance to her partner's sperm. When a mother has not been exposed to a man's sperm for that long, her immune system ramps up against the invasion of the father's antigens contained in the placenta. This makes for a dysfunctional placenta, which is the beginning of a preeclamptic condition in the mother."

"Poor Sadie. I had no idea." I was looking forward to Sadie's birth, but I'm also nursing the thought that a pregnancy begun in a test tube to accommodate a transgender man would end up needing technology to complete it.

Before induction even begins, we use the Bishop score, an assessment of the mother's cervix, to predict its success and speed. Scores for the cervix's length, position in the pelvis, effacement, dilation, and the baby's station in the pelvis are added together for a grand total; when the total exceeds eight, the cervix is said to be favorable for induction. Sadie is at a three.

"Why don't you get your things and go meet Sadie and Jeff at San Francisco General? They are going to be in for a long induction. She's not even effaced yet, so this will take days."

ॐ

The next day is Eid al-Adha, a three-day festival in the Islamic calendar, and I don't want to miss it, *especially,* I think, *to spend it with a transgender family.* The two major holidays for Muslims are Eid al-Fitr, falling after the fast of Ramadan, and Eid al-Adha, or Feast of the Sacrifice, coming two-and-a-half months later and coinciding with the yearly pilgrimage to Mecca.

As the tradition is recorded, the Prophet Abraham, who had prayed for and was granted a righteous son, is commanded in a vision to sacrifice that son thirteen years later. Abraham reveals the vision to Ismail (or, in some traditions, to Isaac), his son, who replies, "O my father! Do as you are commanded. You will find me, God willing, among those who are patient."

Abraham then places his son face down, on his forehead, so he will not have to bear looking at his face while sacrificing him. Satan approaches Abraham twice to try to dissuade him from completing the divine call to action. Abraham throws seven stones at the devil, so intent is he on submission to his Lord.

Likely sweating and trembling, Abraham raises a sharpened tool, when God suddenly calls to him, "O Abraham! Thou hast been true to the vision." As a prophet, he is compelled to answer God's call and turns around to respond. When he turns back to the grisly work at hand, he finds that a white, horned ram has taken his son's place. "Thus indeed do we recompense the virtuous. Truly this was the manifest trial." The English biographer of the Prophet Muhammad, Martin Lings, relates that the horns of that ram were kept inside the Ka'aba until it burned down in 683.

*Qurbani*, the Arabic word for "sacrifice," has a root meaning of "to be close to someone or something"; sacrifice does not come through giving up the lesser things. Abraham is initially asked to sacrifice his son, not a lowly ram. Yet in that offering, there is an exchange, an opportunity to grow in intimacy with the One to whom he was offering.

ᔥ

San Francisco General Hospital, now called Zuckerberg San Francisco General Hospital, is the county hospital. Serving mostly low-income and undocumented patients, there are translating services for more than twenty languages. The teaching hospital is staffed twenty-four hours with nurse midwives, and all the medical residents must go through an obstetric rotation with these midwives. Consequently, they have one of the lowest C-section rates in California. Therefore, when I walk into Sadie's room to check on her I am not surprised to see two brown bottles of herbal tinctures in front of her.

"How's it going?" I ask her. "You brought in herbs for the induction?!"

"No, the midwife here gave me these to take. They put a pill in my cervix, and she said these would help it to work." Cervidil, a drug that helps to ripen the cervix before contractions start, is often inserted at the beginning of an induction, especially to first-time mothers, like Sadie, who enter labor with no cervical effacement or dilation.

"Well, it looks like you're not feeling any contractions yet," I say, glancing at the fetal heart monitor screen spitting out a constant ticker tape of uterine activity and baby's heart rate.

"Oh, Shannon, I'm so bummed we didn't get to birth at the birth center."

"Next time!" I say. "I think you should treat this as you would early labor, ignore it and get some rest. Call me when the contractions are closer to every five minutes, or when they start the

Pitocin. I'm thirty minutes away without traffic." I direct this last part at Jeff, as he will likely be the one calling me. I notice that he looks less comfortable here in a space where his transgender status is less familiar, even in the heart of San Francisco, and where the uniqueness of their family dynamic is on full display—each resident and nurse commenting on the baby's paternity. To deflect any unwanted attention, he is overly gracious to the staff and eager to appease, unlike the assertive Jeff I had seen at Sage Femme. I recognize that feeling—I too often overcompensate to deflect attention away from the unusual combination of my hijab, English name, and white skin. I make eye contact with Jeff and feel an odd sense of solidarity.

ॐ

At 4:30 in the morning, I am jarred from a deep sleep by Jeff relaying the progress of Sadie's labor. His South African cadence makes it sound as if he's narrating a soccer match. "And now they are four to five minutes apart. Lasting a minute, and wonderful, she's just finished another. They've been this way for an hour. We are ramping up!"

Arriving back at General, I find Sadie on all fours on the floor, her hospital gown doing nothing to cover her backside. Jeff concentrates on keeping the fetal heart monitors in place, while her doula gives her ice chips and rubs her back. Sadie is in active labor now, so I suggest she move to the shower to help with the building, intense sensations. Sadie loves that idea and bolts upright, waddling toward the bathroom, the rest of us trying to keep up: doula dragging the IV pole, Jeff unplugging monitors, and me offering a steady hand.

Unplugging the monitors sends alarm bells down the hall to the entire team of nurses and residents, who rush en masse to the threshold of the bathroom door, their nervous energy palpable. As my hand holds Sadie's, I try not to roll my eyes. For all the progressive policies of San Francisco General, the simple ability to read a labor by its emotional landmarks and physical signs has been relinquished to the authority of the blinking screens of fetal heart-rate monitors.

"She wants to get in the shower," I tell the wall of faces staring at us incredulously.

"She can't get into the shower; she's on Pitocin and her IV cannot get wet. We also need to keep her on the baby monitor so we can see how the baby is handling the Pitocin," lectures the nurse while her coworkers nod in agreement.

"Then shut it off," Sadie says. "Just shut off the damn Pitocin. I'm getting in this shower whether you like it or not!" Another contraction begins and clears the air of our disagreement. We all cool our heels and wait.

Once the contraction dissipates, Sadie continues, "If my contractions slow down, I'll get out of the shower, and you can restart it. Just give me half an hour." My heart breaks seeing her having to negotiate the terms of her labor; as if being in labor wasn't enough, she now must bargain for basic comfort measures.

"Fine, but I want you out in thirty minutes so we can monitor the baby again," says some anonymous resident who hasn't even introduced herself. This time, I don't hide my rolling eyes.

Half an hour later, Pitocin-less, we are still in rollicking labor. "Baby, you need to get out of me nooooowwwwwwwwww!!!" Sadie meets her labor with the same brazen nature she greets everything else in her life with. Her hips sway as the water from the shower head washes over her nipples and belly, likely providing the stimulation her body needs to make its own oxytocin, the hormone that elicits and sustains uterine contractions, which the pharmaceutical in the IV drip attempts to replicate. Her doula and I, her boxing coaches ringside, sit on the bathroom floor, offering water, a cool washcloth, and small words of encouragement. Jeff is in the adjacent room, alternating between snoozing and hovering by the bathroom doorway. He doesn't say much. Like any partner, he seems concerned and even a little detached, but I wonder, *Did he feel a throb in his uterus, a desire to be in Sadie's shoes, a longing for what could have been? Does his manhood feel manufactured after witnessing the height of a woman's functional prowess?*

೮⊃

Once we get her dried off, she decides to rest on the bed for a while, and the nurse takes the opportunity to reattach the fetal monitors. Before long we are pushing with each contraction, and the resident and nurse midwife are gloved up, hands folded, watching from the end of the bed. Jeff rejoins the team at Sadie's side, and she reaches for his hand, squeezing it mightily with every push, his thin bones collapsing and face grimacing with each effort.

The average first-time mom, without an epidural, can push for two to three hours. Sadie takes the full amount of time. The sun is now high in the sky and streaming through the windows, giving all of us renewed energy and focus. It's a new day.

It's also Eid. I now know I will not make the Eid celebrations with my family. I will miss my friends in their finest clothing, will miss the piping hot meat stews and fresh flatbreads. Salek will wake up to the Eid gifts I had wrapped before I left and ask where I am. I try to push the thought out of my head to be present with this labor, but a lingering sadness remains. Eid in America is already an effort; you cannot buy Eid decorations at Target or watch an Eid movie to get into the spirit. No one in this labor room will wish me an "Eid Mubarak."

"I see hair!!" announces the nurse midwife, standing behind the young resident ready to deliver this baby.

The next contraction grabs Sadie, and she squeezes Jeff's hand so hard, his knees buckle. His nephew, or son, or niece, or daughter is about to be born, but rather than looking like an excited uncle or dad, he looks like a sleepy onlooker. With the next push, Sadie lets out a crescendo of a growl, followed by an ecstatic sigh; by the tone of that sigh, before I even hear the baby cry, I know that she has delivered. Labor is a symphony, and the conductor has just gently set down the baton.

The resident cuts the cord immediately and lifts the baby up to Sadie's chest; its legs and arms flare out in a startle response, a bloody, screaming five-pointed star. Sadie is sobbing, her glasses fogging up. Jeff removes them so she can see her hard-earned prize. "What is it?" he asks. I find it strange that the biological sex is the first thing he asks about, since that is so clearly not a determinant in his own expression of gender, but old habits die hard, and we are all curious.

"It's a boy!!!!! A beautiful, sweet boy!" Sadie laughs in delight and kisses the boy on his warm, billowy cheek, pausing to drink in his scent. "Do you want to hold him?"

Jeff is mute, but nods.

"Can you help Jeff to hold the baby, Shannon? He doesn't have much experience," Sadie asks. I walk over to the bedside to show him how to nestle the head in the crook of his elbow, the arm curving beneath to support the spine, the other arm providing a full cradle, and I take my first glimpse at this miracle baby, curious to see whom he resembles.

"What's his name?" I ask.

Without hesitation, Jeff looks straight into my eyes, his own eyes glistening with pride and love. "It's Avraham, the Hebrew name for Abraham."

Everything stops. I am alone in the room, alone with God. On this day of Eid, the day we celebrate the sacrifice of Abraham, a Jewish baby boy, conceived in a lab by his uncle's sperm and his mother's egg, his father a transgender man, is now named after the very same patriarch. It's as if God is turning my head to direct my attention away from one thing, the thing I thought I was seeing, and turning it toward what is, what is beyond my beliefs about Him.

In the years since my conversion, perhaps my own mind had become hardened with rules, had acquired a self-righteousness, had forgotten the purpose of the spiritual quest I had initially embarked on. As with birth, it can be easier to follow the rules, like no IVs in the shower; going beyond the rules—residing in that uncertain gray area of an unknown—takes presence and attention, wisdom. In asking Abraham to sacrifice his son, God is asking him to not only go against the external rules about homicide but also go against the internal dictates of a father's own heart.

The rules can blind. I do believe that gender is binary, that God is the only nonbinary, and that whichever gender God assigns us is His perfect design. However, my beliefs about Jeff—his choice to take hormones and grow a beard, to relinquish all the power and beauty I equate with being a woman and exist as something different from divine assignment—I think God is asking me to look past all of that to the shared humanity of His creation, not my ideas about His creation. When we rigidly identify with the rules of a religion more than its spirit, we risk missing the forest for the trees; if compassion for individuals exists, we can see the brilliance of God's creation, a verdant forest breathing life into the rules of religiosity.

"That's a beautiful name," I say as silent tears spill forth. Usually at births, my rule is that I can't cry more than the parents are crying. It's awkward otherwise. But these tears are different; they're mine, washing over my sacrifice, making room for God outside of the margins of my own small beliefs. On Eid, we are asked to make a sacrifice for God, just as Abraham did. In practical terms, goats, lambs, and camels are sacrificed the Muslim world over, kept in backyards, named, and fed until the day of Eid. The comforting confines I had placed on the Divine are what I'm sacrificing on this day's altar.

I hug them both and walk to the parking lot, hoping to catch the last few hours of Eid, as I recite the prayers repeated on this day: "Allahu akbar, Allahu akbar, la ilaha illa Allah, Allahu akbar, wa lillahi al-hamd. God is the greatest, God is the greatest, there is no god but God, God is the greatest, God is the greatest, and to Him belongs all praise."

ॐ

Thirteen years later, in a community hall, a female rabbi carefully unrolls a scroll of the Torah handwritten in Poland in 1920, smuggled out before it could be intercepted by the occupying Nazi force, and stands next to the boy named for our shared prophet, Avraham. Sadie has indeed become the nervous and doting stereotypical Jewish mother; like a butterfly she flutters from person to person, making sure they are oriented to the space and the morning's program. But when she sees me, her wings slow and she hovers in her hug, squeezing me with gratitude until, like that Eid morning, she finds my hand and doesn't let go.

"Shannon, you came! I didn't know you were going to come. I even made sure there is halal food for you just in case! Can you please, *please*, say something during the ceremony?" Not a public speaker, I feel my stomach tighten at the request, only softened once again by Sadie's heart-shaped face and gap-toothed smile. I nod. It's been thirteen years since I've seen Sadie, now a single mother, and Avraham, but the bond we made that Eid day has persisted despite time's march, as has her commitment to the Jewish faith. Here we are at her son's bar mitzvah without Jeff's presence, her original link to Judaism.

While the ancient bond between midwife and mother may not be altered by time, the Jewish faith in Oakland, California, appears vulnerable to it. As I look around, I note the widening chasm of our paths. Next to me, a lesbian couple with their young baby, one of them wearing a yarmulke. Behind me there are several transgender men with prayer shawls draped, their artificially induced beards scraggly on their soft jaw lines. There are half-shaved heads, tattoos, and hair dyes of every hue.

The sacrificial lamb appears to be the very core of traditional faith itself; a submission to God's will appears absent to me, the community room packed with individualized sexual expression clothed in ancient religious garb. It's as jarring to my senses as Judy's explanation of Sadie's pregnancy was over a decade earlier, although this time, rather than feeling a personal apprehension,

95

I feel a universal apprehension. Will the traditional values of faith stand up to the progression of time? In the decade-plus since Avraham was born, midwives have rallied to erase gendered language from their lexicon, carefully replacing *mother* with *birthing person*, *breastfeeding* with *chest feeding*, *birthing women* with *birthing folk*.

Avraham, now a young man in a dapper linen suit with golden hair, recites from the Holy Torah, his voice cracking as he does. These ancient notes once emboldened the Israelites against the maniacal Pharaoh, who employed magic and extreme forms of state censorship and violence to retain his grip on power and shape his constituents' views on reality. It was the Children of Israel, those called to follow the One God, who conjured up the king's insecurities; they feared God alone and could see the limits of Pharaoh's worldly power, so he ordered all the male babies of the Israelites to be killed. Yet unlike some midwives of today, the midwives of the Old Testament took a committed stand for women and their babies in brave acts of civil disobedience. The Torah relates, "The midwives however feared God, and did not do what the King of Egypt had told them to do; they let the boys live."

Avraham finishes his recitation and completes his bar mitzvah. To claps and singing, the attendees hoist Avraham in a chair above their heads; even though many appear as men, they have the strength of women, and the chair wobbles. To balance himself, Avraham throws out his arms and legs, resembling the five-pointed star he was at the moment of his birth.

# CHAPTER 6

*More than shade under a tree*
*On a sunny day in Tennessee*
*More than I love me,*
*I love you.*

—Kareem Salama, "More Than"

Judy always calls me in too early. Clearly this mom is not in active labor, but it's two in the morning and I find myself back in the Arabian Nights of Judy's birth stories.

"So, this guy was such a jerk. His girlfriend is in labor, he's laboring with her, but soon he gets bored, and he calls his OTHER girlfriend to come and take over as labor coach! And Shannon, the laboring mom didn't even care. It was the weirdest birth I've ever been to, and I swear that is why I don't do home births anymore, too many weirdos. Plus, I hate going through people's stuff to find things. Who would want to have to go through someone's underwear drawer?!"

Silence is coming from the Pink Room. Contractions are so mild and infrequent, we don't hear them, and I want to go home to wait out the early labor. Even Judy is impatient, drumming her lacquered nail extensions (how does she manage to do cervical checks with those nails?); she finally caves and sends the two of us midwifery students back home, rare for the social extrovert Judy.

I drive back, east over the Bay Bridge, around the lighted lamps of Lake Merritt, up the hill, into my garage, to fall into the sweet warmth and darkness of my bed, so much better than the half-lit dining area of the birth center and Judy's stories puncturing any sliver of stillness.

*"Does that make me crazy? Does that make me crazy?"* Judy's ringtone, the Gnarls Barkley song "Crazy," jolts me straight up in bed. It's 5:30, just two-and-a-half hours after I closed my eyes.

"You better come quick, Shannon. Marissa's water just broke and it's really swinging into gear."

ℬ

It has been nearly four years of studying midwifery, a humbling experience requiring an inconsistent schedule, juggling last-minute child care, countless sleepless nights, and navigating relationships with the pregnant moms, often years older and dollars wealthier than me, while wearing hijab during a time when groups like Al Qaeda and ISIS have marred the reputation of Islam for many Americans. My discomfort and insecurity seem an expression of Dubois's double consciousness—a constant awareness of how they, the majority, perceive me, the visible minority, supplanting my own experience as a Muslim woman. It is different from my everyday encounters at the library or grocery store. At its core, midwifery is the work of intimacy, of knowing communication styles, of recognizing the need for a well-timed joke or expression, and the art of building trusting relationships while maintaining professional boundaries. Or as one midwife told me, until the baby is born, a midwife belongs in the trenches with that woman and her partner. In a time wrought with distrust of Muslims or even visible religiosity, I want my mothers to know, in this battle at least, I am on their side.

The fumbling of a novice exacerbates this feeling. Mastery begins without muscle memory or instinct. It would be decades before I would adroitly place a Doppler on a contracting mother's firm uterus to be rewarded with the instant readout of a baby's heart rate or slide my hands along her pregnant uterus and have the image of baby's position pop into my head, clear as a sonogram. There is so much to synthesize in the study of midwifery—a pelvis, baby's position, the strength or not of contractions, postpartum emotions, suturing, hemorrhaging—that the gradient alone sheds many an eager student along the way.

Now, I have two births remaining until I sit for my licensing exam.

Four years of apprenticing have taught me my strengths and weaknesses, more of the latter than the former, so that now, nearing the end, it feels more like the beginning, my boots hardly acquiring the dust of the trail. After all, like Imam Malik, the great scholar of Islamic jurisprudence, said, "Half of knowledge is knowing what you don't know." Of that there is still plenty.

ॐ

I reverse out of the garage, head back around the fading street-lights of Lake Merritt, and drive west across the Bay Bridge, the Bay Bridge before the majestic, winged retrofit of its eastern span, when cars continued to weigh down and cruise right over the section, its steel spine arching like a cow's, that collapsed during the 1989 Loma Prieta earthquake. I am on that exact span this morning, though now there is nothing but calm—the sun begins to rise, and the still waters of the bay reflect back the pubescent pastels of the maturing day.

I'm listening to a Muslim country music singer, born in Ok-lahoma, his twangy voice sprinkled with Arabic words giving me a dizzying sensation, a different kind of double consciousness, sort of like being lost in your own city—I know where I am, but I don't.

*I come from miles and miles away, from a far and distant place/ But I pray every night to dream of the light of your face.*

He's singing about the Prophet Muhammad, continuing a tradition amongst Muslims to express their deep love of the Prophet ﷺ through verse and song, an art form that's flourished in all languages that Muslims express themselves in.

The country music lyrics catch me off guard, and I find myself blinking back tears, when I notice the time—twenty minutes since Judy's call. I press my foot on the accelerator, passing the sweeping views of Nob Hill and Coit Tower across the bay to my right, and grab my prayer beads from around the rearview mirror. I put the first bead between thumb and forefinger, my left hand guiding the car to the Ninth St. exit. "Allahuma salli ala Sayyidina Muhammad," my lips flutter with the invocation: "O Allah send your prayers on our Master Muhammad."

As I exit the bridge and sail through the stoplights of the still sleepy Mission District, I recall another bridge, one all souls will one day cross.

After waiting forty years in a shadeless hot plain, the sweat of the crowds rising like a filling bath tub, our bodies, resurrected along with our souls, will await their eternal destination. Before us will span another bridge, crossing not the azure and frigid water of the bay but the boiling pits and raging fires of Hell. Before Dante ever depicted the fiery crossings of this inferno, Imam al-Ghazali vividly described the terrifying scene in his book on death and the afterlife. For some, the bridge will be sharper than a sword and thinner than a hair; for others, wider than the new eastern span of the Bay Bridge, the widest in the world. The bridge will widen and narrow in proportion to each person's earthly deeds; there will be the elect who pass like lightning, others galloping with the speed of a horse, and some crawling on hands and knees or creeping along on their bellies.

Cross it we must, though, and so with what can only be a racing heart and stilted breath, we will take our first precarious step onto the bridge. Ahead, we see physical bodies and their souls spilling over the sides; Angels of Hell await them with hooks and grapples that resemble thorny bushes. We can hear the tortured screams of those who have tumbled. We take another step.

Suddenly, from what sounds like the other end of the bridge, we will hear a familiar voice, "O Lord! My community! My community! Deliver! Deliver!" It is the voice of the Prophet Muhammad, full of concern for humanity and his community, beseeching his Lord, our Lord, to grant us salvation eternally.

ॐ

Each Sunday, we gather to sing a poem in praise of the Prophet Muhammad at Taleef Collective, a third space founded by Usama that's neither mosque nor home. Volunteers serve sweet Moroccan mint tea in colorfully etched glasses that the young children vie to collect, stacking them precariously—Leaning Towers of Pisa in miniature. We sing the poem "The Shimmering Light," burning oud as we do, sweeping its sweet smoke, which will linger for days on our hair and clothes, toward our chest. The community's melting pot is reflected in the recitation, a unique Northern California take on a Yemeni poem, the drum section a combination of djembe drums and duffs, circles of bent wood covered by tanned and taut sheepskin, Moroccan melodies taught to us by an Irish convert, an audible R&B influence in the singer's voice, and some English songs peppered throughout. It is the sound and mood of the Muslims in the Bay Area.

The lines of poetry we recite in Arabic are in fact a birth story.

The first lines of the poem begin at the beginning—with the very conception of Muhammad ﷺ. On the day the parents of the coming prophet wed, a woman named Qutaylah saw the bridegroom walking past her house. Qutaylah was the sister of a convert to Christianity, a rare thing in sixth-century pagan Arabia. Christians and Jews in the Arabian Peninsula held the belief that God's final messenger would be forthcoming from the tribes surrounding Mecca and Medina, an Arabian prophet they sensed was so near that they would feed encroaching armies, just in case the last prophet was amongst the interlopers.

That notion could have been playing through Qutaylah's mind as she noticed a radiant and ethereal light emanating from and enhancing the already handsome face of Abdullah, the bridegroom. Could this be the prophet her brother always spoke of? The light on his face was surely irresistible.

Qutaylah boldly called out to Abdullah, "Take me here and now as your wife and you will have as many camels as have already been sacrificed."

But when Abdullah passed by her the very next day, she searched his face, yet remained silent. When he asked her why she did not propose the same offer to him as she did yesterday, she said, "The light that was with you yesterday has left you today."

Qutaylah's ultrasonic vision detected that the prophetic light that had been in his loins and reflected on his face was now transformed into the building blocks of another.

જી

Marissa, the woman in labor I am driving toward, was also pretty certain of her conception dates. Midwives spend a lot of time talking about the day of conception, the very beginning, so we can arrive at the end, the expected due date. Sometimes it's anybody's guess, between the breastfeeding toddler's frequent night wakings and dad's busy work schedule, the days all blur together. For others, in fact for many Silicon Valley types, conception is a well-timed event, synced with ovulation temperatures and mucus charting, their phone pinging them to alert them to their fertility *right now*. Marissa was one of the former. Her towheaded and exuberant toddler required all of her attention, and her husband, a chiropractor, ran a busy practice on the Peninsula, just south of San Francisco. She preferred to mark her days by yoga classes and farmers markets. However, of the first day of her last menstrual period, a benchmark date, Marissa was confident. Midwives use this day and Naegele's Rule to then calculate the due date—adding a year, subtracting three months, and adding seven days onto the first day of the last menstrual period: "midwife math."

There was a Memorial Day picnic, Marissa told me, and she wore white jeans that she distinctly remembered kept her from enjoying the juicy fruit kebabs. I went with it, adding a year and subtracting months and days to arrive at 280 days later as the due date of her baby.

Ultrasounds, the twentieth-century alternative to Naegele's Rule, when performed in the first twelve weeks of a pregnancy, are accurate at predicting due dates. Embryos develop in a predictable sequence in the first trimester; by week five there is a tiny sac, at week six there is a galloping heartbeat, and by week eight there are arms and ear buds, physical landmarks spotted on the ultrasound that aid in dating a pregnancy. Marissa didn't want any of it. She did not want high-frequency ultrasound waves penetrating the layers of skin, muscle, amniotic sac, reflecting back an image of her coin-sized baby. Declining an ultrasound is not an uncommon choice amongst midwifery patients, especially those who are, or are married to, chiropractors. She knew she was pregnant, and to her, that memory of the sunny May picnic was just as accurate as the ultrasound dating.

$$\wp$$

*And when Aminah was pregnant with him*
*She did not complain about anything that befalls pregnant women*

*For Gentleness from the Lord of the heavens encompassed her*
*And barred from her all harm, worry, and sadness*

Qutaylah's inner vision did, in fact, pin down the conception date of Abdullah's baby, his wedding night. Aminah, the mother-to-be of the Prophet Muhammad, became conscious of a light within her as her pregnancy progressed, until one day it shone forth so strongly that she could see the castles of Bostra all the way in Syria, a place more than one thousand miles from where she stood. The light emanating from her unborn child would provide solace, as shortly after learning of her pregnancy, Abdullah would die. Now the baby filling out her belly and nudging her ribs would be the most tangible reminder of her short-lived marriage. Despite finding herself a widow, Aminah enjoyed her unusually serene pregnancy.

℘

Marissa did not. Tall, blond and beautiful, Marissa worked part time as a model. One rainy day, she was in Ghirardelli Square shooting a spread for maternity clothing. Her belly, round and soft, contrasted with the rest of her slim and leggy body, a turtle's shell on a cat. Colorful umbrellas were incorporated into the shoot, which Marissa had to manage while balancing her very pregnant body on stiletto heels—in the rain. It wasn't a wise combination. Later that evening, I received a phone call from Marissa's husband, Tony. While on the shoot, Marissa had passed out and ended up in the emergency room. She was home and recovering, but the hospital's bloodwork showed a severe anemia. I chalked it up to her vegan diet, but like the light shining to the castles of Bostra, I should have interpreted it as a sign of things to come.

℘

*She saw in a vision*

*That Allah was going to Honor the Creation*

*Through the pure one who was in her womb, so she Rejoiced!*
*And the time for labor drew near, so she was filled with pleas-*
*ure!*

At this point in the poem's recitation, the seekers at Taleef recite
a formula, "Glory be to God, All Praise be to God, there is no
God worthy of worship but God, God is Great." The pleasure
Aminah felt with the first squeezes of labor elicits from us a chorus of "subhanAllah!," like the "Praise be!" uttered by a gospel
choir at church. The drummers pick up speed, teas have been
drunk, the oud smoke, having fumigated the room, now settles,
and we are all transported to that blessed night of his birth.

Shifa'a, Aminah's midwife, was sleeping when she dreamt of
an almost full moon, growing and becoming more luminous,
expanding so substantially that it was about to fall into her lap,
when a knock on the door awakened her. It was a servant, sent
to fetch the midwife. Aminah was in labor.

ॐ

Marissa is in active labor. In the Pink Room, she paces its length,
unable to find a comfortable spot in a labor that is speeding toward its destination. Judy suggests she try the birth tub in the
corner. I fill the tub, checking the floating yellow duckie thermometer every once in a while to ensure that the temperature

107

does not exceed ninety-nine degrees, the sounds of the running water a soothing accompaniment to Marissa's moans. Tony offers sips of water and bites of fruit, and when it's time to get in the tub, he jumps in alongside his wife to help with back rubs and chiropractic adjustments. It must be working, because after just thirty minutes in the tub, Marissa feels a strong urge to push. She tries a few pushes in the water, but then rises from the tub like a geyser to find purchase on dry land. Her dripping wet body leaves a slippery trail to follow her by.

Still restless, with the next strong contraction, Marissa falls to her hands and knees onto the tile floor. Judy, the other student midwife, and I scramble to put down disposable chux pads and towels to soften the floor beneath her. Yet, as soon as we sufficiently protect the floor and create a soft surface, the next contraction comes, and Marissa lies down on her side. Tony, still attentive to his wife, ignores his own need for warmth, his teeth chattering and shivering, as he moves the blanket to warm his wife.

છ

*And the lights emanated from all directions*
*For the birth of the one given intercession had arrived*

*And before dawn, the Sun of Guidance emanated*
*The Beloved became manifest, honored and protected*

The actual moon was still bright but beginning to set as Shifa'a arrives to the bedroom of Aminah, who is ready to push her child into the world. There were no disposable chux pads to place beneath her, and there was no need for one—for there were none of the usual impurities of blood or amniotic fluid present. Stranger still, Shifa'a notices that the mother does not seem to experience the pain of contractions, but only pauses every few minutes, minus the furrowed brow and lagging spirits. The midwife's heart flutters with a sensation she cannot describe. For eons, midwives have operated by sense—and she intuits something momentous is about to occur. Shifa'a, the first one to touch the last Prophet, extends her hands to help the delivery. She steadies herself with a breath, when out comes the most beautiful baby she has ever seen, the one Aminah names Muhammad.

He arrives with his gaze heavenwards, or in what midwives call a posterior position, the umbilical cord already cut. As Shifa'a picks him up she feels her heart tremble beneath her shirt; moving the precious baby toward his mother, she smells a pure and lovely scent, a heavenly, otherworldly musk emanating from the freshly born baby boy. Aminah smiles as she extends her arms for him, looking for traces of her deceased husband in the face of her son, his fists curled into little balls, all but the index finger of his right hand.

இல

Marissa has finally found stillness.

"Here we go. Your baby is so close, Marissa!" I say, adjusting the sterile gloves that I've hastily thrown on. Marissa's birth is the second-to-last birth I'll need to complete my midwifery clinical numbers. I feel no more a midwife than the baby about to be born, but just one more birth after this, and I will be eligible to take the licensing exam. Reflecting on the progress I've made, I wonder why I don't feel more confident and authoritative. Will birth ever feel formulaic, or will it always be a surprise? One day will I carry a map with me, or will I always rely on a vague recollection of landmarks and the kindness of the locals? Birth is vast, and in the fifty or so births I've attended, I cannot say that I know the arteries of its highways or the dusty, yet scenic, back roads it is apt to take.

"AAAAAYYYYAAA!"

I am snapped back to attention by Marissa's next contraction, my hands drawn to her perineum like a magnet. Judy pours oil into my gloved hand, and as I've been taught, I use the oil to soften the tissues and surrounding muscles to prevent tearing, and, unscientifically speaking, to make slippery baby's passage, which it does—the entire baby flies out onto the chux pad.

Shocked at the speed of the baby's entrance, it takes me a second to grab the warmed baby blanket from Judy—as I rub the blanket up and down the spine, I note that it is the smallest baby I have ever delivered; I could hold it with one hand. Judy and I exchange concerned glances and then quickly get to work.

Grabbing another warmed blanket, Judy and I rub the baby some more to stimulate breathing—it hasn't cried yet.

But Tony has. "Is it a boy or a girl?" he asks through tears, attempting to look beyond our hands at the genitalia. "Marissa, it's another girl!!"

I look up to Marissa's face, but she doesn't have the look of utter relief that most mothers feel at the culmination of birth. The baby finally cries, loud and insistent, but due to the baby's size, Judy worries that something else may be going on with the baby.

"Cut the cord," she whispers to me. She's traveled this back road before. I do as I'm told and hand the tiny wisp of a baby off to Judy. Tony follows her to the infant warmer. All babies have trouble regulating their temperature at birth; the moisture of the birth quickly evaporates and cools their core temperatures. Skin-to-skin contact with mother or father usually offsets the cooling, baby's temperature soon settling to within one tenth of a degree of mom's or dad's. Smaller babies with less subcutaneous fat have a difficult time keeping warm with or without the comforting skin-to-skin contact.

But I can't pay attention to what's happening with the baby. Marissa has entered a physically vulnerable state, for when birth goes wrong, it is usually at this moment that the body—shed of the baby, tired from the exertion of labor, in need of nourishment—can refuse to release the placenta or clamp down on the uterine arteries to prevent bleeding. If ever the eye of a midwife is needed, it is now, the third stage of labor. But Marissa is not bleeding.

"Tell me when you feel a contraction," I tell her. "You still have to birth your placenta. Everything is fine with baby girl. Judy is just keeping her warm and checking her out, as she is on the small side." It strikes me then that Marissa has never measured small; in fact she always measured a little big. *It's probably the vegan diet,* I think to myself.

But Marissa doesn't seem concerned with the baby or her placenta. "Shannon, something is kicking me! There is another baby in there!"

"No," I smile indulgently. "I'm sure it's the contraction you are feeling. Let me check to see if the placenta has separated and is just sitting there."

"No, Shannon." Marissa grabs my hand, preventing me from reaching the cord. "Something is kicking me. There is another baby in there!" Tony rushes from his newborn daughter back to Marissa's side.

"Okay, let me grab the Doppler and see if I can find another heartbeat." I'm humoring her; not one part of me believes there is another baby in there. Yet as I reach for the Doppler, the lanes of this birth become clearer—small baby, anemic mom, no ultrasound, unconfirmed dates—I have not traveled this road before, but it's becoming clearer where it's headed.

*Boom, boom, boom, boom.* 142 beats per minute, the Doppler reads out. My eyes widen and meet Marissa's equally wide eyes. There is no mistaking it: that is another baby's heartbeat.

112

ℬ

*And his light filled the horizons*
*It encompassed the entire Universe*

*The icons of idolatry have been torn down*
*And the edifice of idolatry has crumbled*

At this moment, the spectacular moment of the birth of God's final messenger, the entire gathering stands in reverence, hands raised in supplication, sending prayers, along with the angels, on the soul of our Beloved Prophet ﷺ.

As I stand shoulder to shoulder with the other women, I remember Aminah at this time, her third stage of labor completed, her midwife slipping quietly from the room to offer privacy to the new family. Midwives call that first hour after birth the golden hour, a time of heightened hormones that elicit intense pleasure and bonding for both mother and baby.

Nearly a millennium and a half later, the immensity of Aminah's birth and our bond to that baby who would one day become our beloved Prophet resonates as palpably as the drum beat thrumming in my ears, the swish of the women's skirts as they sway to the beat, the heavenly scent of oud. It's as if we are all still basking in that golden hour.

ℬ

I turn to Judy, at once knowing what to do and yet desperately seeking a guide—is it okay to cross this border? Judy walks over with more blankets, directing the other student midwife to keep an eye on what we are now calling Baby #1.

A brown sticky substance is oozing onto the chux pad. Meconium. Baby poop. Meconium can be a sign of fetal distress, and I grab the Doppler to check the baby's heartbeat. A steady 143 beats per minutes. Not a stressed baby.

"It's breech," says Judy. Breech babies, entering the world hind end first, often release meconium due to the pressure on their stomachs during the birthing process. With twin births, it is common to have the first baby head down and the second breech, an elegant way to share space in the uterus. A breech birth—it's like I'm driving on the left-hand side of the road. I can drive, but everything is backward.

With the next contraction, the meconium now wiped away with a clean gauze pad, Judy's hunch is confirmed. Instead of a wrinkly raisin, I'm looking at a smooth peach, the buttocks are coming, and fast.

Tony is at Marissa's side as she lets out a fierce "UUUUUNNNHHH!" He is bewildered as the second baby emerges, as dainty as the first. Her insistent cry seems to say, *You didn't know about me all this time, but I'm here now, so pay attention!* Already at birth, their personalities distinguish what their looks cannot.

Marissa's beautiful face (even after pushing two babies into the world, she could grace a magazine cover) shifts from concern to bliss. We all take her cue and stop to marvel at the miracle that has just transpired. On an ordinary Tuesday morning in the Mission District, deep in the caverns of the Sage Femme Birth Center, in the Pink Room, where there was supposed to be one new life, two lives emerged—the secret of their creation a secret only their Creator could keep.

"Twins," whispers Marissa as she strokes her daughters' wet heads, her full lips turned up in a joyous smile.

"Twins," whispers Tony, bewildered. He begins to mutter calculations under his breath. "But we only brought one car seat, we will need two strollers, and that's three girls…"

He did not plan for this much abundance.

ဆ

The day that the Prophet Muhammad ﷺ was born, the beds of kings were turned upside down and the animals spoke.

His mother, Aminah, though, simply put her newborn to her breast, laid her head back, and rejoiced at the arrival of her son. Shifa'a occasionally would have felt Aminah's uterus to ensure its involution and also would have given her something warm to drink. The world would never be the same after that blessed Monday in Arabia—but that particular morning Aminah simply dozed with her baby, and Shifa'a went back home to a house full of chores—the sacred slipping back into the ordinary.

ॐ

I finished my clinical numbers with Marissa's births, Baby #2 counting for my last birth and annexing more, yet unexplored land to my internal map of birth. The girls, identical twins, grew up happy, their mother's milk supplemented with a vegan formula created by their parents. When I saw them for their six-week postpartum visit, the family squeezed in with a double stroller, diaper bags everywhere, and Tony chasing after their toddler while trying to bottle-feed one of the twins—the sacred secret of the unknown twin now mingled with the ordinary struggle of everyday parenting.

ॐ

On the hallowed day when our souls will traverse the bridge, our resurrected bodies drenched in sweat from the inferno beneath and the stress of our eternal predetermined end before us, that sacred destination paramount to our focus, we will hear above the din of the fire's pops and cracks a voice, its tones and tenor perhaps harkening us back to our brief stint on earth, to our mother's sunset call directing us back home, to a daughter's simple "mama" or a lover's whisper—a singular voice, ordinary, simple, everyday, now elevated to the sacred, "Oh Lord, Deliver! Deliver!" An intercession between us and our Lord, the beloved voice of our Prophet ﷺ will plead for our deliverance from the blaze below. He will be prostrating before God as he intercedes,

116

the same position he was born in. It is said that he won't raise his blessed head until the community of believers is saved.

Birth is a glimpse of a little bit of the sacred commingled with the ordinary. Some births, however, give us more of the sacred and less of the ordinary, more of the sacred than we could ever have imagined.

# CHAPTER 7

*Your body is not a lemon. You are not a machine. The Creator is not a careless mechanic.*

—Ina May Gaskin, American midwife

Back in St. Louis, in the weeks and months after my conversion, I had attended a weekly *halaqa*, or study circle, on Friday nights with a group of fifteen to twenty women in their early twenties. Sarah Khan, a medical student attending Saint Louis University, led the group, her keen intellect allowing her to deftly direct our discussions toward some of the deeper fault lines within the burgeoning political frontier of post-9/11 America and our place in it as "hyphenated" American-Muslims.

Case in point: In the week or two after September 11, 2001, *Time* magazine featured Osama bin Laden on its cover. To begin our group's discussion for the night, one young woman holds up a copy and asks us, "What do you see when you look at this picture?"

A beard? A turban? A terrorist? A Muslim? She slowly moves the cover around the circle, and his small brown eyes glare at us.

*"Nur,"* says the woman. "I see *nur*."

Still unfamiliar with Arabic terms, I innocently raise my hand for clarification. "What does *nur* mean?"

With an unapologetic gaze, she looks straight into my eyes and replies, "It means a spiritual light."

Spiritual light?! The man that Washington, D.C., is currently hunting in the caves of Afghanistan for the murder of thousands of Americans has a "spiritual light"? I feel unmoored as I look around at the innocent scene that is playing out in living rooms all over the world—women surrounded by plates of food, our feet curled up on couches, bodies in repose, emotional cups filled; a scene that minutes before had filled me with relief that this female activity crossed religious lines now fills me with dread—these women see *nur* where I see cold and calculated death. Did I make a mistake?

I look questioningly at the woman, who responds, "The war with the Russians had left such chaos and disorder, destroying Afghanistan's social net and culture. Women were frequently the victims of rape, both by the Russian soldiers, and in the Afghan public schools, where young men taught women simply a few years younger than them. Food was scarce and expensive. The Taliban gave Afghans back a sense of safety. What may have seemed to the outside world as a strong-armed response provided order in the turmoil the Russians had left."

Sarah notices my continued discomfort and steps in. Of course, no one agrees with the horrific acts of 9/11, she says, but the Machiavellian response of the Americans doubling down on a country so devastated by centuries of war, without providing the Taliban clear proof of Bin Laden's guilt, which they requested as a condition of handing him over, is not only absurd but evil because of the innocent lives that will be lost.

Uncomfortable with the quickly polarizing events following 9/11, Sarah keeps her paint in overcast and steely shades, somewhere between black and white.

In birth, however, the only two paints on her palette are black or white. After those cozy Friday nights in St. Louis, Sarah begins a residency in obstetrics and gynecology, and I begin attending births in bedrooms and bathtubs—two divergent paths in the same forest.

∞

Shortly after qualifying for my license, we're reunited in the Bay Area, finding ourselves sitting in its largest mosque, the Muslim Community Association in Santa Clara, California, designed out of the carcass of an old Hewlett-Packard office building. At their annual women's conference, we are to co-present a session entitled "Hospital vs. Home Birth: Pros and Cons."

I mentally review my index cards as I set up the chairs: C-section rates skyrocketing, effects of epidurals on breastfeeding rates, safety of home birth, postpartum care, and on and on. It feels more like I am preparing for a television debate rather than a breakout session to a crowd of eight at a local women's conference.

If I were a midwife in any other highly developed nation, this contest would be unnecessary.

My research is based in part on the work of Melissa Cheyney, a midwife and medical anthropologist, as well as the author of one of the largest studies on planned home birth in North America. She contrasts the difference between the American system of maternity care and that of other developed nations, such as Germany, England, and New Zealand, where "obstetricians in these systems almost exclusively attend high-risk mothers who require specialized interventions, while midwives offer high-quality, individualized, and lower-cost care to the majority of women."

Indeed, her study found that in nearly seventeen thousand home births with North American midwives, the cesarean section rate was 5.2 percent, compared with a national average near 32.1 percent. America's high cesarean rate, according to Cheyney, "result[s] in maternal death three times more frequently than do normal vaginal deliveries."

Not only that, but these cesareans are expensive. The U.S. spends more per capita on health care than any other developed nation, without subsequently improved outcomes. Low-tech midwifery care is far less expensive than a hospital birth, but with better outcomes for both mother and baby.

When I look up from my index cards, I see a familiar smiling face, Zahra, her belly covered in clearly expanding polka dots.

"Zahra! I didn't know you were expecting! I'm so glad you are here!"

Months earlier, I had met Zahra at an open house for a local farm-based preschool. Standing in line to pet the cow, Zahra, in her expressive way that I came to adore, let out a huge screech as the cow stepped toward our spot in the fence and tried to steal her apple.

"I am expecting, and I really want to know more about home birth," she says in hushed tones. I'm not sure who she is hoping wouldn't hear.

"You're in the right place," I reassure her as I help her find a seat.

Sarah bounds in, her hijab, as always, pinned neatly under her chin, her sparkling smile doing more for her face than any rouge or mascara, and she takes in the room.

"Salam alaykum, everyone," she says, asserting herself right away. *Just like a doctor,* I think, *to take control first thing.* "I'm going to talk about hospital birth, and then Shannon will talk about home birth. Then we will take questions from the audience."

She sets her diet soda in front of her, the table otherwise absent of notes or aids. My handwritten pile of index cards seems sophomoric in comparison. Looking around, I count more than double the number of registered women in the room. Are they curious about home birth or repelled by it?

Sarah explains the hospital routine, complete with pain relief, a television to watch until it's time to push, and a private postpartum room.

As soon as I start talking, everyone straightens up, especially Zahra.

"Midwifery care offers mothers individualized care that allows for you to make informed decisions in a trusting relationship with a midwife. I bring everything a delivery room in a hospital is equipped with, except an anesthesiologist and access to immediate surgical intervention. But if you're a healthy pregnant woman with no risk factors, your birth shouldn't require medical intervention. Your body was created to do this; just like you digest proteins, carbohydrates, and absorb the minerals in your food without outside intervention, your body too can grow and birth your babies without external aids."

As I look around the room, I see wet eyes simply acknowledging the mother's ability to birth, a balm. I shouldn't be surprised; when women ask me to attend their births, they don't come with a set of numbers and statistics. Women who have had unnecessary separations from their babies at birth long to feel the immediate pleasure of their babies skin to skin; women who have been told their pelvises are too small to ever have nonsurgical births want to appeal that edict; women who want to affirm the mighty and miraculous ways their bodies, unaided, birth their babies— these women don't come with a stack of numbers jangling in their heads; they come with their hearts desiring a different entrance into motherhood.

"But is it safe to have your baby at home?" asks one young Somali woman. "My mother says that a lot of women died back home because they didn't give birth in a hospital. Why wouldn't you have your baby in a hospital?"

"Exactly!" exclaims Sarah as she slams her palm onto the table for emphasis. "This is 2009, not 1909. We don't grind our own wheat any longer, and we don't have to have our babies at home either. There is no reason to have your baby at home when you can comfortably and safely have your baby in a hospital with an epidural. We don't have to turn back the clock."

Shuffling through my index cards, I find the stats and quickly rattle them off.

"No, it's not 1909. It is 2009, and our current cesarean rate is hovering around thirty-three percent in this country. Marsden Wagner, a perinatologist out of UCLA and an advocate of midwifery care, says that 'having a highly trained obstetrical surgeon attend a normal birth is analogous to having a pediatric surgeon babysit a healthy 2-year-old.'"

Sarah rolls her eyes. "I would rather have a highly trained doctor monitor the well-being of me and my baby, even if it's not always necessary. When things go wrong in birth, they can go wrong quickly."

"But our maternal mortality rates are rising," I counter; "in fact, the rates have doubled since 1987! It is the least safe place in the developed world to have a baby, and this isn't because of midwives or home births; less than two percent of all births in America take place outside of the hospital."

Sarah and I proceed to volley back and forth as we answer the many questions that follow. When a mother asks how important nutrition is postpartum, Sarah takes a swig of her diet soda and says, "Very."

જી

Zahra's living room is a Target ad with a Palestinian twist. An enlarged art deco poster of Jerusalem's Dome of the Rock hangs in a gallery wall next to framed swatches of her grandmother's traditionally embroidered dresses. A collection of vintage tea-pots, some spray-painted robin's egg blue, sits atop her media cabinet. Her throw pillows, pops of yellow and red, are perfectly fluffed, no small feat for a house with two active children. The smell of freshly baked cookies completes the cozy effect.

I haven't been in a house this familiarly decorated since I last visited my mother. Most of the Muslim women in my practice either have very little furniture, an attempt to emulate the few material goods possessed by the Prophet Muhammad, or en-deavor to recreate a traditional Arab or Pakistani sitting area, the golds and bright colors extravagant to my Western eye. Zahra's house is the first house I have been in that draws inspiration from both Pottery Barn and the patterns and palettes of the Middle East. I settle right in on her sectional and pull out my chart.

"Zahra, I'm so happy to be here. I love your house! Today we are going to go through your health history, the current preg-nancy, and your first two births. I'll review your lab work and then we will listen to the baby!" She hands me a plate of mini chocolate chip cookies still warm from the oven. "Why don't you start with your first birth."

It is the first chapter in our story together, her health history an outline to the narrative of how she arrived here, on her sofa with a plate of warm cookies, detailing the plot line to a midwife taking notes. The burgeoning belly in front of us is a chapter not yet written, though we have an idea of the direction we want it to take.

"Oh, you mean with Pitocin Princess?! Well, I was young and knew nothing about birth. When I was thirty-nine weeks pregnant, she told me she had to go out of town and that I needed to be induced. I didn't know any better and was getting tired of being pregnant, so I agreed. No one told me anything about the side effects of Pitocin—that it could make the contractions harder than those my body could produce, or that I could even refuse the induction. I mean, there was zero medical reason for her to get me into labor. After the first hour, I begged for pain relief. They gave me an epidural and that was fine. The labor lasted forever, though, and I was exhausted when I came home. I had so many problems with breastfeeding. My husband wasn't any help, and eventually I developed postpartum depression. All Pitocin Princess offered was a prescription for an antidepressant and told me to quit breastfeeding." Zahra's voice wavered at the memory.

Chapter 2 of Zahra's story involves the same characters, though the mother has developed a stronger voice and directs the storyline.

"For my second birth, I told her I didn't want an induction unless it was medically necessary. Around my due date, I went into labor. I stayed home for as long as I could, but by the time we got in the car, I asked my husband to call ahead and make sure the epidural was ready and waiting for me! It was. But as soon as they gave it to me, literally within minutes, Abdullah was born. I was so mad! Why didn't they check me first to see how dilated I was? No one even offered that as an option. If I knew I was so close to delivering, I would not have taken the epidural! I felt robbed of something I had prepared for. Why didn't they want to help me achieve the birth I desired?" Now, anger creeps into Zahra's voice.

By all objective standards, Zahra's births were successful—healthy mom, healthy baby—but in the subjective telling of them, something is amiss. Zahra did not leave her births with a renewed spirit, a knowledge of the female body that she could pass down to her children; rather, she walked out of the hospital defeated and unheard, her voice an afterthought in the grand narrative of modern maternity's theater, and, even though she left with a newborn in her arms, empty.

⁃⁃⁃

Ina May Gaskin, the mother of the modern American midwifery resurgence, was a young and idealistic woman in the late 1960s with two braids hanging down her back and bell bottoms to match. She delivered her first baby in the back of a bus. While the mother labored, the caravan of hippies traveling from San Francisco to Tennessee had all pulled off to a rest stop, and Ina May offered the little she knew about midwifing women—she pulled the shades on the van, encouraged affection from the woman's partner, and offered her supportive presence. A few hundred miles later, the entire caravan once again paused their travels to stop at a local grocery to weigh the community's newest member on a produce scale—a mere five pounds, two ounces.

Known simply as The Farm, the woods of Tennessee marked the caravan's end—and the commencement of one of America's largest unofficial studies on out-of-hospital birth. By 1974, Ina May and a few other women were delivering up to thirty babies a month, far outstripping the birth rate of the nearest county hospital. A kind local doctor befriended the midwives and would come out to assist them in cases that stumped the self-taught women on The Farm.

To their surprise, Gaskin and the other midwives didn't have their first cesarean section until birth number 187. A study comparing the outcomes of births on The Farm with physician-attended births concluded that for low-risk women, "home births attended by lay midwives can be accomplished as safely as, and with less intervention than, physician-attended hospital deliveries." The Farm midwives' cesarean rate between the years 1971 to 2000 was 1.4 percent.

Hardly one generation embedded into American culture, and Zahra is already countercultural.

ॐ

But one week after her due date, Zahra looks for some kind of intervention. "I just want this pregnancy to be over! I can't believe I've been pregnant this long. Like, I didn't even know it was possible to be pregnant this far past the due date. Everyone keeps asking me when the doctor scheduled my induction for!"

We are all piled on the love seat in Zahra's family room, she and her very pregnant belly, her two curious and rambunctious children, and me, all of us highly anticipating the first contraction. At Zahra's birth, I will no longer be the student in the passenger seat but the driver who knows the way. I have obsessively been checking the ringer volume on my phone each night and running through emergency scenarios and how to address them as I have drifted off to sleep. In my dreams, there are trios of mom, baby, midwife, all of us basking in the glow of a job well done.

Her son helps me measure the baby and find its heartbeat as I reassure Zahra about the normalcy of going past the due date. "It's more of a guess date; no one can pin down the exact time of conception. Take some time to enjoy these last few days of being pregnant. And distract yourself with a project or a walk in nature!"

Distract herself she does; in the next few days Zahra hangs a gallery wall in her living room, and then one in her family room. She makes cinnamon rolls from scratch, covering them with a tea towel and setting them in a warm place to rise. Another vintage teapot is spray-painted robin-egg blue.

The morning of her labor, Zahra rests on her couch. Each time she stands up she feels an immense pressure. I had told her that for mothers who have had babies before, the soft tissue and bones of the pelvis yield to the weight of the baby so that contractions often feel like pressure at first, rather than like the tightening of the uterus as felt in prior births. Mothers soften like stone fruit left on a sunny summer countertop, their sweetness and ease developing with time and experience.

At four in the afternoon, she gets up to make chicken and vegetable chowder for her family's dinner. Feeling strong, she packs up the kids and heads out for a couple of errands, the craft store and the library. Her son and daughter would have new books and art projects to keep them busy while Zahra nurses the new baby.

By 7:30 that evening, Zahra knows that tonight she will meet her baby. She calls me to report infrequent but strong contractions. I tell her to hydrate after each one and to go to bed soon in order to be rested for labor. I try to do the same, but my nerves jump to and fro. The responsibility of the health of mother and baby lie with me alone this time, on my training, my skill set, the readiness of my hands. I place my birth bags by the door, the oxygen tank resting on its wheels, the blue chart balanced on top. I am as ready as I ever will be. The camel is tied, and the rest is now up to God.

At midnight my phone rings. It's Zahra's mother, Amal, who despite being a mother of six has never been in labor herself. Newly emigrated from Palestine, her first was a cesarean section, and all five subsequent babies were also surgically delivered.

In her beautiful Arabic-accented English, she asks, "Shannon! Am I going to have to deliver thees baby? Please come soon, Zahra is having loots of contractions, and she will not move from the bathroom!" I see where Zahra gets her expressiveness. My heart is beating, my breath shallow, the adrenaline doing its work as I jump out of bed, throw on a hijab, and rush into the car.

My grandfather knew the southern Minnesota landscape like he knew the contours of his wife's hand. He knew from the sunset what the next day's wind would be, and from the moon, how cold. He could tell the amount of rainfall by the corn's tassels. Highway 880 is my landscape, its darkness enveloping me as I sail down its wide lanes, the streetlights brightening my car in regular intervals. I know the 880 so well that I can recite its exits in order. It's the main artery from which I map out the Bay Area. Tell me where you live, and I'll tell you which exit to take. Like my grandfather, my work has given me an internal landscape of my external surroundings.

As I turn the blinker to exit the freeway, it dawns on me: Zahra and I, midwife and mother, are resurrecting a knowledge of birth that has skipped at least three generations on American soil for me, and less than one for her. Zahra's mother, born at home herself, could not pass on an embodied knowledge of birth to her daughters, her scarred uterus remaining silent.

৪০

The porch lights are on and the door unlocked as I lug my birth bags and oxygen tank into the house. Breathless, her mother rushes me. "Shannon, she is going to have the baby in the bathroom. She will not move from there! Can you get her to move? The baby cannot be born in there." She says all of this while tugging at my elbow, leading me down the hall to the bathroom.

Zahra, in her bathrobe, is half kneeling on the bathroom stool; waves of nausea after each contraction prevent her from venturing off the cool tiled floor. I grab my Doppler out of the bag and perform midwife acrobatics, lying on my back and reaching my hand between Zahra's half kneel to assess the baby's heart. *Woosh, woosh, woosh.* I see Khaled, Zahra's husband, who hails from Gaza, and Amal's shoulders drop a couple of centimeters, relieved smiles lighting their faces. Now they are ready for the birth.

"Let's move this party to the bedroom. Zahra's going to feel so much warmer, and I will bring a bucket for her to throw up in if she needs." Khaled springs into action, lifting Zahra to a standing position, his hands beneath her arms as if she was one of his small children, not his wife with the basketball belly. She wraps her arms around his neck as they slow dance their way to the bedroom. *What gets the baby in gets the baby out*—the famous saying of Ina May Gaskin is being enacted by the tenderness between Zahra and Khaled. It is a moment she will recall fondly in the retelling of her birth story.

"There's so much *pressure*!" Zahra cries as she sinks, kneeling again, her arms draped over her bed.

"Would you like me to check you? Maybe all that pressure means it's time to push," I offer.

She nods in assent, and between contractions we help her up onto the bed. Twenty minutes later, she finally makes it there. Very gently, I assess her dilation, internally thrilled that the assessment is all mine, no preceptor to double-check my findings. I don't have to go very far before my fingers meet the hard and rounded edge of baby's head. Once there, I glide them past the head to be sure there is no cervix left. There is. She's eight centimeters dilated.

"You're eight! It's not quite time to push, but the baby is very low, so the pressure you're feeling will only increase as the contractions push him or her further out of the birth canal. Let's try a few contractions laying on your left side to see if that doesn't alleviate some of the pressure."

Now Khaled and Amal are reenergized. Maybe it's my sterile gloves, the confirmation that labor is nearing the end, or my frequent auscultation of the baby's heart, but it seems to me that their skepticism and fear of Zahra's choice to birth at home have given way to a new ownership of the experience. The birth is as much theirs as it is Zahra's. Khaled holds Zahra's hand and helps her every move while Amal hands me my Doppler and warms the baby blankets, clutching them close to her as she awaits the arrival of her grandchild.

A midwife's ears are attuned to the sound of the contractions toward the end of labor, listening for the primal grunts of a mammal bearing down with the contractions. After thirty minutes on her left side, I hear it.

"It might be time to push. Would you like me to check you one last time to be sure?"

"*Yesss!* There's so much pressure. I can feel baby's head, I think!"

So can I, the head is so low, only two of my knuckles fit. My body fills with excitement and anticipation, a huge smile slaps onto my face, and I announce, "Your baby is right here, Zahra. Whenever you're ready, it's time to push."

Before the baby is even born, I think, *We have done it,* the ageless duo of mother and midwife working together to preserve and uphold the marvelous ability of a woman's body to birth her child. I held the space for Zahra to bring her baby to this precipice. And she, through sweat, vomit, tears, and lots of determination, has arrived at the implausible; all that stands between her and relief are a few strong pushes, the Chinese finger trap of birth; the only way out is through.

It is a piece of knowledge we have both traveled far to reclaim.

It takes mere minutes for the shadow of baby's hair to appear, and one final push for the entire baby to enter the world. The delivery is so smooth, no pause between head and shoulders, just one slippery descent onto the soft landing of the very bed in which she was conceived. Truly, what gets the baby in gets the baby out.

Amal rushes to the screaming baby, her tears flowing as she puts the blankets to use drying the baby.

"Hey, that's my job!" I tease. But she doesn't hear me. Drying her granddaughter, it is as if she is reliving a moment she never had—an instinctual knowledge about the possibilities and miracles of birth come back to her, and she knows just what to do. Carefully minding the still attached umbilical cord, she hands her granddaughter to her daughter, a cycle once broken, repaired.

"Alhamdulillah! Allah bless her. It's a girl, ya Zahra. You did it! Alhamdulillah." All praise is God's. I sit back and observe three generations of females tasting the euphoria of a birth undisturbed.

"She's beautiful! I did it! Shannon, I really did it!" As colorful and expressive as ever, Zahra bursts into a hearty round of tears, beginning a chain reaction, until there isn't a dry eye in the room.

*You did it! We did it!* I think to myself. Mother and midwife, traveling new terrain to reclaim old knowledge, the simple knowing that women's bodies were designed to birth their babies.

ॐ

Back in that St. Louis living room full of food and women, Sarah was zooming out, looking at modern political events with a wide lens, giving texture and context to a narrative not found on CNN or Fox News, a lens I believe she and her colleagues could do well to view midwives through.

Beyond statistics, knowing how to give birth outside of technology and operating rooms is a knowledge humanity cannot afford to lose; it's a knowledge birthing women and their midwives, like Zahra and I, are preserving one precious birth at a time. Midwives, far from the ignorant and dangerous women that doctors often depict them as, are experts in birthing humans in a context of love, safety, and warmth—a beginning all humans deserve. And they do so with the hope and intention that, as the midwives of Ina May's generation coined, "Peace on Earth Begins with Birth."

# CHAPTER 8

*The wound is the place where the light enters you.*

—Rumi, as interpreted by Coleman Barks

Pregnant again, but this time in Oakland, too far for Renee to travel, I have found my next midwife. Another Judy.

Incongruously a former nun and a member of the ultrafeminist Boston Women's Health Collective, this Judy penned the home birth section in the first edition of *Our Bodies, Ourselves,* the revolutionary manual on women's health and sexuality.

In fact Judy was such a pioneer of midwifery in the seventies that when she wanted to learn about birthing babies, there were few experienced midwives to tutor her, obligating her to also apprentice with a hardy Vermont country doctor who, like the country docs of yore, still attended women in their homes in the muddy back roads of Vermont.

From him she would learn no-nonsense skills that had kept generations of American mothers and babies thriving, like evaluating the circulation of a newborn by the color of its gums and the utter importance of delivering babies in a room warmed, whether by woodstove or space heater, to at least seventy-four degrees Fahrenheit.

She likes to say she is a mother and a woman dressed up as a midwife, a nod to how she views the partnership between us—

two women, equals, supporting one another in reclaiming knowledge of the female body. With a shock of white hair, an effusive warmth, a thick New England accent she often employed to recite lines of poetry, and a philosophical bent that deepens our interactions, Judy exudes irresistible charisma—a cross between your favorite English professor and hippest aunt.

"Shannon, you look beautiful. I hardly recognize you without the hijab! Najeeb, it's wonderful to meet you, and of course, little Salek! How are you?!" she says patting our child's head and embracing us one by one as she makes herself at home.

"I'm so happy you've chosen to work with me. It's a real treat when one midwife trusts another. You are the one who has the most authority here, not because you're a midwife, but because, as the mother, you are the one most invested in the health of you and your baby. I am here to encourage that, but you are ultimately going to determine and know what is best for the family. And you know what, we are going to have a great time!"

The largesse of her personality and her total confidence put us all at ease. We are going to have a great time.

෨

"Shannon, take a big breath and then exhale deeply," Judy says, her hands, the joints already knobby from arthritis, framing either side of the baby's head. As I exhale, she pushes her hands into the bowl of my pelvis and attempts to move the presenting part from side to side. Grabbing her ever-present fetoscope, the one she's had since 1979 and *they don't make 'em like this anymore,* to listen to the baby's heart, her brow furrows with a concern left unsaid.

Wielding a fetoscope, a special stethoscope used to listen to baby's heart rate in utero, Judy shuns the use of a Doppler, saying she prefers to hear the actual heartbeat of the baby, not the heartbeat through ultrasonic waves. As she hands me the fetoscope, I close my eyes to focus on the sounds. *Boom, boom, boom.* It is intimate and near, like hearing my own heartbeat when I sink beneath the still bathwater.

I notice that the fetoscope is positioned higher than usual, at my belly button as opposed to nearer my pelvic brim, and instantly Judy's furrowed brow makes sense. During my own pregnancy and birth, I try hard to turn off my midwife brain, preferring to rely on mother's intuition and stay out of my head; otherwise each new sensation becomes a cause for analysis and concern. Plus, it's exhausting to try to midwife myself, so I happily hand the reins to my midwives. But there are some things you can't unknow.

"Is the baby breech?" I ask Judy.

"It is. You're already 36 weeks, so we are going to have to work quickly to get the baby to turn by the time you're term in one week. First, I want you to do inversions every day. Take an ironing board and put one end on the couch and the other end on the floor. Hang out upside down for fifteen minutes. Next, go get some acupuncture as it is proven to help turn breech babies. One of my daughter-in-law's babies was breech and what worked for her was putting a pack of frozen peas on the baby's head! Baby didn't like that, so she swam down and away from the cold peas right away!"

"I'll do all of those things, but Judy, if the baby doesn't turn and I go into labor, you will still deliver me breech, right?" A scenario like this constituted one of the reasons I had chosen Judy; a variation of normal could, by lesser midwives, be shipped off to the hospital but, by skilled wise women, be handled safely at home. Observing the Bay Area community of midwives, I had seen that the ways they practiced were as diverse as the women they attended; some had very strict protocols and ended up in the hospital as much as they stayed at home, while others were stereotypically crunchy but lacked the skills to keep women at home safely. Judy adeptly walked the narrow line down the middle.

"I have attended dozens of breech births. Breech used to be considered normal. We would handle it carefully, but before ultrasound was the norm, sometimes it would just happen! I want you to do all you can to turn the baby, and then we'll talk. You are a good candidate for breech, you have what they call 'a proven pelvis,' this baby isn't more than seven pounds right now, and you are both healthy."

&

If the baby remains breech, I know my options are limited. In 2000, a large study found that breech babies delivered vaginally had a one percent increased risk of death in the first six weeks of life over breech babies delivered via cesarean section. Despite some problems with the study—mainly that it's difficult to randomize anything in childbirth—most major hospitals and, more importantly, medical schools began shuttling all mothers of breech babies to the operating room instead of first offering the opportunity to birth vaginally.

When a baby descends headfirst, the bones of the skull mold to the shape of the mother's pelvis; in a breech birth, however, the soft buttocks can slip out of the cervical opening before it is fully dilated, potentially causing the head to become trapped in the mother's body. Practitioners familiar with breech presentations have developed techniques to avoid such a devastating situation; some insist that mothers adopt a hands-and-knees posture for delivery; others employ a hands-off approach, not touching the baby until the entire body is out, giving the mother's body time to dilate. Yet others have the mother slide her buttocks to the very edge of the bed so that the body can dangle, giving more pressure and gravity to the heavy head of the newborn, encouraging descent and dilation.

But since 2000, no one is learning any of these techniques; medical students are no longer taught the art and skill of delivering a breech baby. Only doctors with one foot out the door to retirement, who had worked in obstetrics long before the breech study and were trained to view breech as a variation of normal, would allow me to attempt a vaginal breech delivery, even in a hospital.

Either this baby decides against coming feet first, or Judy will have to brush up on her breech delivery skills.

℘

First thing in the morning and last thing before I fell asleep, after every inversion, after the walk down the hill to the park, even in the middle of conversations with friends, I find my hand following the contours of baby's back to the presenting part—does it move back and forth easily, as if it's attached to a neck, or does baby's whole body shift as I wiggle the presenting part?

"Stop feeling the position of your baby! How is your baby ever going to turn if you are constantly touching it, anyhow?" Elham, my constant park companion and Chicagoan friend who, loyal to her city, tells it straight.

She's right, I think, as I push my stroller and very pregnant belly past Lake Merritt and back up the hill, but why is this little one stubbornly in the three to five percent of all babies who are breech at term?

While Salek naps, despite a determination not to midwife myself, I peruse a volume of Anne Frye's *Holistic Midwifery*. A prolific author of midwifery textbooks, Frye is known for her minute attention to detail and her informed yet creative solutions to pregnancy and birth complications; for the stumped midwife alone at a birth in the middle of the night, her textbooks serve as a stand-in colleague with a wealth of experience.

The hard lump of baby's head rubs against my rib bone as I read through the many reasons babies can remain breech at term: pelvic tumors or cysts, poor abdominal tone, short or tight umbilical cord, placenta previa. None of these apply. Then, in her atypical approach to diagnoses, Frye discusses breech "from the baby's perspective." One passage strikes me:

> Breech and transverse positions symbolize comfort for the mother and the baby, as the position places the baby's head near the mother's heart.

I rub the sore spot on my ribs beneath my heart; it reminds me of another sore spot, an older one, one that I hadn't considered for some time.

℀

The cornfields are shorn of their summer bounty. The moon lays bare the pokey remains of last season's harvest. My grandfather, a naval pilot who returned from World War II to study agriculture and play basketball for the University of Minnesota, guides the Buick through snow-packed roads to Midnight Mass. Grandma hums a Christmas carol off tune as she applies her red lipstick, a saturated shade that turned her deep-blue eyes unseasonably bright; it's a shade, she would later tell me, not to leave home without. She keeps her leather gloves crossed neatly in her lap. The forced air warms our noses and feet against the brittleness of that winter in Minnesota. It's here with my paternal grandparents that my sense of home, my sense of being seen, forms.

My brother and I are a world away from my father's house in a characterless suburb of Minneapolis, where he has full-time custody, and from my mother, who is building a new house on new land with a new family and a new name. Here, with our grandparents, we're in Fitzgerald's middle-west, *a city where dwellings are still called through decades by a family's name.* When I'm in "town," the block with the grocery story and the café where the men gather to talk about today's corn and bean prices and the women gather later to gossip in the back room over fresh donuts and coffee cake, I only have to say my last name, and not only is it recognized (*Oh, you're Mike's daughter!*) but, by the smile on a stranger's face, I know it's respected and loved.

When we arrive at Mass, my aunts, a few nursing babes in their arms, and uncles are stacked next to their children. Like any good Catholic family, ours takes up three pews. Warm smiles greet us—the patriarch, matriarch, and two stragglers— and squirming children are elbowed to scoot over and make room. The starched collar on my formal velvet dress, picked out by my grandmother, scratches as I genuflect and make the sign of the cross. I notice the fashionable, tasteful dresses my aunts had chosen for my cousins, and my throat tightens. So desperately I want to be like my cousins, flanked by two rosy-cheeked parents, their sibling squabbles not overlain with divorce's edge, arriving to Mass certain about who they are, where they belong.

Candles light the entire building, and an organ heaves familiar hymns from upstairs. The choir, which includes one of my great aunts famous for her singing voice, belts out the Latin verses. The nativity play begins with a procession from the back of the church. Two of my cousins star as wise men. We giggle as they gamely attempt to maintain their comportment and studiously avoid eye contact. The lingering smell of frankincense penetrates the church.

Mary sits alone on the stage, looking perplexed by all the attention. In that country church, where three generations of my family have been married and buried next to dozens of family members, I too feel alone. Divorce, so common amongst even Catholics, falls on our society like a heavy rain on a windshield, but we often forget its effects on the individual, a lone raindrop that falls on an eyelash, felt and singular. For me, divorce meant an introverted father, who smoked pipes and read books in his library while coping the best he could with single parenthood, and a perpetually distant mother, the two eventually cleaving into new families, I adrift and solitary in their wake. For now, I slip my small hand into my grandmother's warm, gloved hand and float in her regal wake as we make our way down the aisle and back home.

☙

I have read that clutter in the hallways, doorways, and entryways of the house can cause a breech baby. Out goes any hint of miscellany; toys and outgrown clothes exit in a steady stream of garbage bags. Still breech.

Squats can help a baby to turn head down. I do fifty squats after each prayer in order to open my pelvis, inviting the larger sphere of a skull. Still breech.

Music played at the pelvis has been shown to interest babies and prompt them to orient their ears near the music. We play recordings of Qur'anic recitation for baby. Still stubbornly breech.

Salek begins to shine a flashlight over my pelvis and sweetly whisper, "Swim to the light, baby. Swim to the light."

Still breech.

I heave my pregnant self to the office of Jill, my beloved acupuncturist, who in her essence is a healer. Petite with an energetic presence and focus to match her hip outfits pieced together from boutiques in the Haight district, Jill brings to the acupuncture table a personal level of therapy, a sense of heart-to-heart connection with a girlfriend. As she feels my pulse and looks at my tongue, Chinese medicine's version of diagnostic labs, she manages to narrow down exactly what's going on.

"Your kidney qi is depleted. You're trying too hard. What is worrying you?" She doesn't move her hand from my wrist, waiting for my answer with a compassionate, honest gaze. Her questions have me sobbing before the needles are even in.

"This pregnancy feels so different, Jill. On one hand, I feel vibrant and glowing, but deep down, I feel afraid. But I can't pinpoint the fear."

As she begins to swab with alcohol each of the points she will be needling, she asks, "Do you think it's because you've given birth before? Maybe you're afraid of the birth itself? Sometimes knowing what you're in for is worse than facing the unknown."

She takes the increased flow of tears as a yes and continues, "Why don't you try doing some birth art to express what's going on? Words don't always get to exactly what's playing in the subconscious. You could make a collage, on one side put words and images of your ideal vision for the birth and on the other put words and images of everything you're afraid might happen at the birth. Expression helps to move energy too."

The needles are all in now, including two in my pinky toes specifically meant to turn this baby, but I've already got what I came for. I close my eyes and let the qi and the tears flow, and then, the startling thought arises : *What if it's a girl?* It's like the needles removed my resistance to the true kernel of my fear—I know why this baby is breech.

In my practice I have observed that women's bodies often communicate through physical ailments: unexpressed anger as a urinary tract infection, a stubborn anemia in a mother who always puts herself last. In this case, stunningly, it isn't just my body conveying a message; it is the baby within my body alerting me to an unmet need.

Deep down, I'm afraid that I won't be a good mother to a girl. How will I raise a daughter who will one day raise a daughter who will one day raise a daughter, and on and on down the Russian doll of lineage, when I myself haven't had a mother in the home, my maternal memories embalmed in the amber of early childhood years?

There on the table I remember another acupuncturist's office that I had visited before enrolling in midwifery school. In this Marin County acupuncturist's office, twelve eager midwifery students gather around the regal midwife and author of the introductory textbook *Heart and Hands Midwifery*, Elizabeth Davis. Her angular cheekbones and long blond hair could have launched a modeling career, but her ethnic flowing wardrobe tells another story.

"This path requires deep internal work," she begins as we sit cross-legged, our heads following her as she sashays the length of the room. "If you aren't working on your own healing, how can you expect to heal someone else?"

She stops in front of me and looks straight into my eyes, holding my gaze. "In order to be an excellent midwife, you *must* work from your own wound!" I didn't understand it at the time, but her advice stuck, like gauze on an open wound, no matter how much I wanted to rip it off.

Only now, with needles opening the energetic channels to rotate the upside-down baby, do Elizabeth Davis's sage words resonate—in order to succeed as a midwife, and apparently as a mother, you must work from your wound, the edges of which fit perfectly around the baby's head, a tender snuggle beneath my heart.

෮

At the following prenatal, I'm desperate to stop all the breech exercises. Judy must read it on my face as she hugs me and says, "How's that baby? Head down yet?"

"I don't know. I've been doing absolutely everything to get baby to move! What else can I do?"

"Why don't we have a feel?" Judy offers, skipping right over our usual tea and snacks, getting straight to the exam.

I lie down on the couch; Judy kneels at my side and immediately extends her hand to my pelvic brim. Cupping the presenting part between her thumb on one side and her fingers on the other, her other hand finds the body and rests there. Moving the hand at the pelvis back and forth, Judy feels with the other hand to see if the body moves with it, just as I had been trying to do these past two weeks.

"Yup, head down. Good job, Shannon. You can go ahead and have this baby anytime now!"

If only the baby *would* come anytime now. The due date comes and goes. This child clearly has its own ideas about how this is going to go.

Judy gives me homeopathic pills to help stimulate my uterus, small, sugary pills to be taken every day for three days. Thursday night, ten days over my due date, I take my last dose. Between this Groundhog Day pregnancy that doesn't seem to have an expiration date and the weeks of attempting to turn a stubborn upside-down baby, my body feels like a dud.

The next morning, as I stumble to the faucet to wash up for prayers, I am fully awakened by my own water breaking, a faucet

149

of its own running down my legs onto the cold tile. For a full minute, I blink at the growing puddle at my feet. Even though I am heavily pregnant and ten days overdue, I don't quite believe it. As I'm toweling up the mess, I feel a sharp cramp in my abdomen. *Indigestion,* I decide as I stand on my prayer mat facing Mecca.

I try to lie back down, but the sharp cramp keeps coming, rhythmically and periodically, making it difficult to lie horizontally. Recalling my dinner last night, I wonder what is upsetting my stomach, ignoring the bulge of the pregnancy. I decide fennel tea and buttered toast will do the trick.

I set the kettle on the stove and look out the window at the Oakland sunrise, its golden rays sweeping across the floor, highlighting the crumbs amidst the terra cotta tiles. With everyone still asleep, and for once no household task beckoning, I am still in my own kitchen. It's in the receptive calm that I let creep in the notion that this indigestion may in fact be labor. Maybe today will be the day…

The contractions accept my surrender and lengthen in response—*Nice to meet you too.* Between contractions, I sip on the fennel tea, its sweetness lingering in my mouth. During contractions, I grab the edge of the granite counter and roll my hips in large circles. It has the effect of spreading the intensity down and out, expanding isometrically to the uterine contraction.

Salek wakes up, and the buttered toast I made for myself becomes his breakfast. The fennel tea is still steaming when Najeeb walks in. "Are you having contractions?"

"I'm not sure; it kind of feels like indigestion. Let me finish my tea and…" I can't even finish the sentence before another rolling contraction begins.

"I'm calling my sister and Judy." Najeeb, now familiar with my early labor denial, begins to manage the boundaries, shuttling off the older child, calling the midwife, filling up the birth tub, which permits me to reenter the internal stillness and surrender of the morning's dawn. I sweep and wash up after Salek's breakfast—the *chop water, carry wood* of motherhood does not pause for labor.

∞

It's been a little over an hour since my water broke, and I am already deep into labor's throes. Each contraction has me grabbing the edge of a shelf, keeping a slight bend in my knees, and circling my hips—an ancient belly dance, the beat of which I can only now distinguish. Salek watches a cartoon, and the noise of it distracts me from the rhythm of my own labor and from that deep internal landscape that is the yin to the yang of my contractions.

I move to the bathroom, the fennel tea taking up precious real estate in my pelvic bowl. In the background, I am aware of my sister-in-law coming for Salek, of Najeeb fiddling with the birth tub, and of Judy arriving. The quickly progressing labor has Judy and Najeeb busy setting things up for the birth, leaving me alone on the cold, hard toilet seat, a stark contrast to the fluid rhythm

151

I had been dancing to my contractions with, and in that difference, the connection to my breath recedes as my brain processes the change, and I feel nauseous.

"Najeeb! Bring me a cold washcloth with lavender essential oil." Somewhere in the recesses of my mind, I am subconsciously midwifing myself and it's pushing me further toward panic.

Judy's brought her student, Lael, to help her with the labor. Lael comes into the bathroom with a preternatural confidence, as if this pain were as easily scaled as the hills outside my door, and squats down, her tall frame squeezed into the small space in front of me. She puts a hand on my thigh and holds the lavender-scented washcloth on my forehead. "You're doing great. Just breathe. You're almost done." Najeeb steps in besides her and rubs my back. They are two pillars relieving me of the need to bear all the weight.

After the contraction Lael places the fetoscope on my lower abdomen and marvels at how low the baby already is.

It is low, because a few minutes later, I no longer feel nauseous; I feel like pushing. Drawn to the oxygen-rich water, as if my lungs are gills, I gracelessly lumber into the tub, causing the water to splash onto the tarp-covered carpet below. I close my eyes and let the water take the tension of my shoulders, returning me to my breath. When I open them, Judy is on the small loveseat across from me, looking like she is taking in a sparkling Mediterranean view; in this repose her face is relaxed, calm, and carefree.

Grantly Dick-Read identifies fear as detrimental to a laboring mother's progress and places the doctor or midwife as the sentry at the door, keen to expel any whiff of fear. He advises birth attendants to maintain three *P*s and three *C*s; patience, peacefulness, and personal interest along with confidence, concentrated observation, and cheerfulness.

Judy combines all six; her spot on the couch could be cheerily occupied for hours while her unflappable smile takes the second stage of my labor in stride. Like a gymnastics coach, she offers tips from the sidelines, "Relax your eyes. Let your shoulders drop," along with gentle words of encouragement, "Yup, that's the way. Beautiful."

Having birthed one child before, I am not surprised by the sensation of pressure from the baby's skull bones between my legs, but it is still only a foothill to the mountain of pushing this baby through my bones. I desperately want Judy to get up and confirm with her gloved hand that this effort will soon produce its intended results, but she is affixed to that spot on the couch.

"I can't do it anymore! I can't!" I shout at her.

She takes in my frustration and smiles serenely without moving an inch. "There's only one way out now."

I want to splash birth tub water on her.

Resigned to pushing this baby out, I close my eyes to try to find that place of prayer and stillness from earlier. I find it. Between contractions, sleep overcomes me, and I lay my head back on the edge of the birth tub, awakened only by the rush of the uterus bearing down, down, down. A few more rounds of sleep and the drill of contractions, and I instinctively reach down to feel the outlet.

"I feel the baby's head!" I announce. No one but me seems surprised.

Not even my daughter. With the next contraction, I hold my breath; diving beneath the wave, I swim past the shore of the self I thought I was, beneath the churning tumult of these giant breakers, beyond the fear of losing my breath to the pressure of the water, and I retrieve her. Together we swim to the surface, a mother and daughter—found.

As I lift her through the skin of the water, I know it's a girl before parting her legs; thick black hair frames her round, placid face. She looks around the room and then utters one single cry, *I'm okay*, before closing her eyes and falling asleep in my arms. In one hour and forty-five minutes, we came a long way. When I gaze at her, the love I feel is singular and hard won, a pursued and rare remedy for weathered wounds.

℘

We name her after both of her great grandmothers, Fatimah Elaine. Fatimah, my husband's maternal grandmother, a descendent of the Prophet Muhammad herself, died before he was born. My grandmother, Elaine, her red lipstick, blue eyes, and strong faith, epitomized all that was good throughout my childhood. Fatimah, also the name of the daughter of the Prophet, was known to be fearlessly loyal; she used to step out with her father and try to shield him, her little body bravely standing between him and the cruel attacks of his enemies. When her mother Khadija died and her father was left a widower, she took exemplary care of him, so much so he used to call her "the mother of her father."

Even before birth, my Fatimah has proven to be "the mother of her mother"; before she has taken her first breath, Fatimah has nudged me to grow. I can still feel the bruises where her head rubbed against the bone in the parabola of my ribs, where she defied the norm to float upside down and swam up beneath my heart to get my attention—*Mom, there's an old wound there; let's tackle it together!* When I listened and acted, she in response corrected course, proving from our earliest beginnings that together we could break cycles of pain with love and attention.

Or, as Rumi says, she showed me that the wound is where the light gets in.

∽

I know my own birth story. My mother's water broke at midnight, and contractions picked up after that. Before they left for the hospital, my father made the proverbial begrudged sandwich. When they got to the hospital, Nurse Pinkie kept shutting the door, blocking my mother's focal point during contractions, an outlet at the nurse's station across the hall. Dr. Pepper delivered me at 9:09 on a crisp January Minneapolis morning.

In my mother's telling, her face alight with the recall, it was easy, without drama or struggle. I have carried glimpses of her delight at the story of birthing me, a nutritious snack when the hunger of missing my mother growled.

There was joy and love before. There is joy and love after.

∽

Once baby is dried off and tucked into bed, Judy decides we could all use a cup of coffee on this fine spring morning and walks down the hill to Café 504. I imagine her return up the hill, the sun shining on her back and that mischievous smile still playing on her lips, balancing our lattes as she bends down every once in a while to pick a bouquet of May wildflowers, replete with California poppies and violet lupine, for the new mom and baby.

She enters my room, bouquet and coffee in hand, opens the blinds, and declares, "At this point in a birth, it's a social event!"

We laugh and sip our coffee, letting the morning's joy retrace the scars of yesterday.

# CHAPTER 9

*…and for the moon*
*We have determined phases,*
*Until it returns to a tiny crescent.*
*The sun is not to overtake the moon,*
*And the night does not outstrip the day,*
*as each swims in an orbit.*

—Qur'an 36:39–40

It's after sunset in East Oakland, the tiny sliver of the new moon dangling above the hills providing no light for my path back and forth over the train tracks but an orientation for my circuitous turns. My phone, like an unanswered child, keeps repeating back to me that I've arrived at my destination, but there is no habitation at the destination. Then, out of the corner of my eye, I see a previously unseen lane between the main road and the train tracks. I turn down it, and there through the foggy mist appears the address from the Craigslist posting, a lighthouse in the darkening shadows of an Oakland night.

Lauren, her height leaving little negative space in the doorframe, her vintage cat-eye glasses two satellite points on either side of her head, backlit in the entryway's light, throws open the door.

"You made it!! I was wondering if you were lost!" Her easy smile and confident voice erases the frustration of finding this out-of-the-way place in a sketchy part of town and puts me in a cheerful mood.

We chat for a while about the educational books I've come to buy from her. She tells me she's a teacher's aide at a Montessori program and highly interested in alternative education but doesn't have children of her own yet. I hand her the cash. She gives me simple directions to get back to the highway and then asks, "Are you a teacher?"

"No, I'm a midwife. Call me if you ever get pregnant!" I say as I smile over my shoulder and head back to the car.

&#8500;&#8500;

A few months later, I get an email from Lauren:

> I remember you told me you were a midwife, and that when I got pregnant I should give you a call! I just got three positive home tests a few days ago and I'm currently 5 weeks along with an estimated due date in early August.

I'm so excited I pick up Fatimah and twirl her around the living room.

It's been nearly a decade since I converted, moved to California, donned the hijab, and adopted all other facets of the Muslim lifestyle—no pork, no alcohol, only halal meat—a decade of almost a cultural anthropological immersion into a foreign country. Yet I've stayed within the borders of California. It's been years of deciding what parts of my pre-conversion life to retain, what to bring into the boat of a religious community not quite itself docked on Western shores, afraid that if I bring too much it will be *Man overboard!* I've let more go than I've held on to, relinquishing customs, or at the very least modifying them, for Muslim dress or diet. Thanksgiving with family requires a separate turkey cooked for us and accommodations to my grandmother's sweet potatoes (marshmallows contain gelatin derived from pork). Fourth of July, my sister is in a bikini at the pool, and I am not, covered head to toe, sweating under the weight of my decisions, feeling as out of place in my family as I imagine an immigrant would returning to his impoverished village after spending years on a PhD in physics at a prestigious university. No matter how zealous the conversion, or how much the present virtue is sought for the promise of a generous future reward, I am human, and as Odysseus in his decade-long quest to return home says, *I have been gone so long it hurts.*

From the very first birth I attended, the hijab, weighing mere ounces, began weighing heavier and heavier, pounds it seemed. As the intensity of the labor rose, so heightened the self-consciousness of permanently advertising my religion via an unavoidably obtrusive head covering. Birth, honest birth, never allows for artifice; it forces me to shake hands with the two sides of myself, one that adopted an unfamiliar faith as a lifestyle, and the other still the granddaughter of a Polish hog farmer and an Irish brick layer, a lover of bluegrass and Kerouac, a wanderer watered on Whitman. Lauren by the railroad tracks belonged to me as much as the veiled women at the mosque.

Was all of this just playacting, the hijab a costume, a gossamer exoskeleton sloughed off carelessly on a backstage stool, discarded upon actualization or when its skin became taut at the burgeoning beneath, or was I really a Muslim, not just comfortable with the choices I had made as a young woman nearly ten years earlier but transformed by the daily drip of forehead to earth, of the traces left by the continual utterance of *la illaha ilallah's* tongue to palate? Does one ever return home from a journey the same as the one who left?

I had yet to fully traverse the rocky waters between my American self and my Muslim self, and it showed up the most in births. Perhaps predictably, given its sharp symbolism in Western culture, the hijab would become a mental focal point for me, a loop of negative thoughts like a flower crown above my head. Is this cloth making them uncomfortable? Do I look ugly in it? Do they think it's unsanitary?

Lauren has emailed me despite the hijab and a part of me wonders if she had even noticed it in the dark of the night.

℘

Lauren's home resembles my aunt Rosanna's farmhouse, interpreted for urban Oakland: vintage Pyrex containers stacked aesthetically in her equally vintage dining hutch, bone broth bubbling on the stove, mystery bulk organic grains and legumes in glass containers lining open shelving, the tile countertop buckling beneath the weekend farmers market haul, and almost an entire sheep's sheepskin sprinkled on the floor and across the back of the couch. There is even a dedicated craft room stocked with yarn and fabric.

The familiarity of the space, in addition to the fact that Lauren was barely pubescent when 9/11 happened, adds a fresh dimension to my interactions with her—there's less baggage around Islam and more bonding over shared values outside of a religious context, around health and living, local and simple, opening up a side of me that didn't always emerge so freely around my religious peers.

With Lauren, America and Islam balance perfectly in the foreground and background, neither one receding nor ascending, the edges legible. Clear. It's like being at an optometrist's office and flipping through lenses—"Clearer, clearer," you say with each snap of the lens, as the blurriness begins to lift.

During our winter prenatal visits, we sit on her (yes, vintage) patinated leather couch with steaming mugs of tea, swapping recipes for ferments and soups. We laugh at her persistent pregnancy craving, burritos from the local taqueria—nearly one a day. "At this rate, you will push out a burrito instead of a baby," I tell her.

In spring, during a mid-pregnancy ultrasound, we learn it's a girl, whom they rapidly christen with the lovely, and very California, name of Juniper. At her baby shower, Lauren bans pink.

"Enough is enough," she says. "I can't stand all this princess shit." Lauren has the mouth of a sailor, and she wields it impiously.

As spring blooms and Juniper takes up more space between us on the couch, we marvel at the odd synchronicity of the centimeters a mother's uterus measures, equaling the number of weeks of gestation, so that by 35 weeks of her pregnancy, Lauren measures 35 centimeters, and so it appears that early August is indeed when Juniper will plant her roots in the Oakland soil.

෨

Islam's calendar calls this August by a different name. Relying on a lunar calendar, Muslims traditionally mark the beginning and ending of the months by the moon's emergence rather than by the staid seasons of a solar calendar, resulting in a yearly difference of roughly eleven days. Today, the majority of Muslim countries use the solar Gregorian calendar for civil and social purposes, reserving the moon's timings for strictly devotional use.

To sync their lunar holidays with the unchanging solar calendar, the Jewish community adds a thirteenth month every third year in a process called intercalation. It's a liminal month, not occurring in reality, only holding space until the next month can begin and sync itself between the sun and moon's timings. This is similar to how we calculate the weeks of a pregnancy from the first day of a mother's period, though in actuality, for two of those weeks, she wasn't even pregnant. Both timings are calculated to meet the needs of modern diaries, schedules, and timetables. In his final sermon, the Prophet Muhammad ﷺ forbid intercalation, thereby encouraging his community to gaze at the night sky at the end of each lunar cycle and sight the birth of the new crescent moon.

In his book *Caesarean Moon Births*, on the importance of sighting the moon to begin lunar months, Shaykh Hamza elucidates a deeper purpose than demarcating time to sight the moon:

> The premodern peoples of the world were oriented to the sun, moon, and stars, and such phenomena connected them with the heavens on a daily basis. Sighting the new moon is a practice that maintains that connectedness.

So every year throngs of East Bay Muslims pack up the family van and wind their way up Grizzly Peak Road in the Berkeley Hills to the Lawrence Hall of Science. Lauren's pregnancy, now in full bloom at thirty-nine weeks, has me concerned about my spotty cell phone reception in the hills. But up, up we go, Salek and Fatimah singing along to Yusuf Islam's "Ramadan Moon" song, their version of my Bing Crosby Christmas carols.

*Moon, Moon, come out soon!*
*We're off to see the Ramadan Moon*
*Clouds shift fog lift!*
*City put out your lights*

*We want to see*
*the Ramadan Moon*
*tonight!*

"Mama, do you think we will see the moon this time?" asked Salek, shouting over Islam's crooning. We had come up the hill the night before, but disappointingly a moon had not been seen and we continued eating and drinking in daylight hours.

"I hope so! Either way, tomorrow will be Ramadan!"

Like midwifery, sighting the moon is considered a communal obligation, so that if one person in a community can fulfill this role, it relieves the rest of the community from an obligation to do so. Each month, the *muwaqqit*, the sacred timekeeper, must go out to a high point in his or her vicinity and await the sighting of the new moon. However, there are some months in the Islamic calendar that find us all *muwaqqits*.

Shaykh Hamza cites the Swiss writer and convert to Islam Titus Burkhardt's description of the excitement around sighting the Ramadan moon in the ancient city of Fez. Burkhardt writes:

On the evening that Ramadan begins, the keeper of the time is not the only one on the look-out. On every rooftop people watch impatiently to see whether, following sunset, the young crescent moon will become visible. First one or two, then a quickly increasing number, espy the fine silver horn on the still light horizon. A cry of joy breaks out, for it was in this month that the Koran was revealed to the Prophet. This joy can be felt throughout the city.

This month elicits a communal crescendo of joy at sighting a celestial body signaling the believer to commence the month-long fast of Ramadan, wherein another celestial body now delineates our days, for from the sun's rising to its setting, we refrain from water, food, and sexual relations. Ramadan, unlike the sighting of the moon, is not a communal obligation but an individual one, upon every man or woman in sound health. For many, it is a time of heightened spirituality, the dulled physical senses giving way to a spiritual longing and closeness.

The Lawrence Hall of Science sits atop a hill with a spanning view of the Bay; on a clear day you can see east to the refineries of Richmond, north to the emerald hills of Marin county, west across the water to the Golden Gate Bridge and the sparkling San Francisco skyline. While our eyes focus on a place on the horizon between Richmond and Marin, the kids scramble over the large fin whale and giant double helix–shaped play structures, their feet crooked into the major and minor grooves. Someone has brought glow sticks for the children, while others pass out homemade cookies and treats; there is a thermos of chai for the adults and one of hot chocolate for the kids. The mood is festive, and a primordial sense of community reigns.

However, we are one of a minority of Muslim communities in America maintaining this practice. Even some Muslim countries no longer use the naked-eye sightings of the moon to determine the start of Ramadan. Similar to the Jewish community, in order to keep their calendars in sync with modern schedules and timelines, Muslims now employ complex calculations available months ahead of time, abandoning the age-old and simple practice of awaiting the uncertain sighting of the moon. The first night of Ramadan is now known well in advance; Eid vacations and party spaces, already reserved.

As the sun sets to the right of the Golden Gate, someone gives the call to prayer, and it echoes off the Berkeley Hills. The children quiet their play and climb down off the dorsal fins and DNA structure. We roll out prayer mats turning our backs away from the bay and our faces east toward the hills to offer the three units of prayer. When we are done, as one body we dash toward the ledge, our eyes fixated on the darkening crimson sky.

The anticipation I feel as I strain my eyes to the heavens reminds me of waiting for Lauren's labor to begin. Although scheduling a labor induction, penciling it in on the calendar, and knowing for weeks beforehand your unborn baby's birthday is convenient, it is also bland. Trusting in divine authority over even the smallest of details, from the first grimace of a contraction to the first day of fasting, engenders a sense of awe that's otherwise lost in the order and predictable schedules of our daily lives—no one can induce the birth of the crescent moon, or a baby; they are born on God's time.

In explaining his reason for his book title, Shaykh Hamza tracks a similar sentiment:

Like a caesarean birth, the early announcements of the lunar months that have historically accompanied a calculated new moon are primarily the result of conforming to the scheduling requirements of modern bureaucratic societies.

"There it is!" someone shouts, and before our eyes, the slip of a moon is born.

It is literally born, emerging from between the clouds as miraculously yet as plainly as when the first wisps of baby's hair emerge. The new moon, a clipped fingernail, a slender eyelash, a sliver of a glow, is, after all the waiting, a manifestation of the Qur'anic statement, "Verily! That is easy for Allah."

It is said that in Ramadan, the devil and his minions are locked up, unable to continue their devious plots and whisperings. No one can predict that moment; it is a metaphysical reality that doesn't care about lunar charts or calculations.

It is Ramadan. Tomorrow we will fast.

ॐ

By the time late August comes, Ramadan is nearing its end, our bodies now used to the fast, our spirits already aggrieved at its departure. Lauren has taught me to bargain with the farmers for the tomatoes they don't sell at the end of the market and how to can said tomatoes. I have taught her that due dates are imprecise, a calculation that 97 percent of the time is totally off, as good as a blindfolded child pinning the tail on the calendar.

Eric, Lauren's husband, calls me right as I am going back to bed. It's four in the morning, and I have just eaten the pre-dawn meal and prayed the dawn prayer. While I have been eating dates and oatmeal and drinking copious amounts of water to hydrate for the dry August fast, Lauren has been having regular contractions.

She is now forty-two weeks and two days, more than two weeks past her given due date. Some years later, the California Medical Board would prohibit midwives from attending women at home past forty-two weeks, an attempt to "calculate" safety that would have the side effect of shunting otherwise healthy women like Lauren into the hospital for inductions. For now, though, we have been trying homeopathic remedies, herbs, acupuncture, talk therapy, anything to get labor going. Now that it's here, it's as if the clouds have parted and I've sighted the crescent moon all over again. Nothing we did or predicted worked to bring on labor—our hands could not part the clouds.

In the *Journal of Perinatal Education*, Judith Lothian sums up the purpose and wisdom of waiting for the natural phenomenon of labor to begin:

> The watchful waiting and the intense wanting of the big day to arrive are all part of nature's plan. When the baby, uterus, placenta, and hormones are ready, labor will start. Additionally, all that preparation sets the stage for an

easier labor and a fully mature baby who is physiologically stable and able to breastfeed well right from the start.

"Hey, Shannon. Sorry to call so early, but Lauren has been having steady contractions for a couple of hours. They're about seven minutes apart now," Eric says.

"Okay," I say, struggling to sit up in bed, knowing I must now preserve my energy for the fast *and* the upcoming labor. "Can I talk with her to get a better sense of what's going on with the contractions?"

Eric puts Lauren on the phone. "What's up?" she chirps, alerting me to the fact that we have not passed the threshold from early labor to active labor.

"Not much; it's four in the morning. I just want to listen to a few contractions to get a sense of where you're at."

As I fall asleep between the contractions, I know that they are not close enough together for active labor; with early labor lasting an average of 20 hours for first-time mothers, Lauren could be at this until I'm eating again this evening.

"You're doing great! We have been waiting for these contractions!!" I tell her. "Let's talk again when they are a consistent four to five minutes apart. You could take a shower now, try to get comfortable on your side and sleep between, or just get up and start your day."

"I'm laying back down, man. This is tiring!" says Lauren.

As soon as I hang up the phone, my eyes slam shut and I fall into a deep sleep.

℘

Through the arched doorway, the late morning sun streams into the dining room, where the table has been moved and, in its place, an azure birth tub has been set up and filled. To keep the heat in, layers of wool blankets and handmade colorful quilts drape the tub, giving it a cozy ambiance.

The birth supplies are neatly lined up against the wall in paper bags, waiting for me to organize them. After taking blood pressure and listening to the baby, I begin the ritual passed down to me from each midwife I studied with: heating pad plugged in with baby blankets warming on top and bottom, resuscitation equipment placed next to the heating pad, placenta bowl lined with a disposable chux pad, the Doppler and gel, anti-hemorrhagic medications, birth instruments and sterile gauze all placed inside the bowl, and a box of non-sterile gloves atop the nearest surface. With every move, my stomach growls, and I cannot help but look at the clock and count the hours until sundown. Will we meet this baby between now and then?

"I'm so tired, but so hungry!" says Lauren, echoing my thoughts. "When can I get in the tub?" She hurriedly bites into a mango and takes a sip of coconut water from a stainless-steel straw between her contractions, which are now coming every five minutes like clockwork.

"Let's wait until the contractions are a little closer together and longer before we get in. The tub really has a way of slowing things down if you get in too soon. Let's try walking awhile."

Eric helps Lauren off the couch, and for the next hour we walk back and forth from the kitchen to the living room.

By the time the sun is past its zenith. Lauren's contractions have responded to the walking by increasing in intensity and shortening their intervals; they are now every three minutes.

I say, "Guys, I'm going to call the second midwife, Bethany, to come now. You know that means it's getting closer! Then, I'll need to take five to pray. I'll use the craft room." I excuse myself and notice that it is not strange for me to tell them this. Lauren nods her assent and Eric, his arm draped over Lauren's shoulders, grins at me over his shoulder as he helps her navigate the corner.

Maybe it's the clarity of the fast, but in that moment, I sense the immigration wall between the two sides of myself crumble, and I don't have to travel much further until I'm home. There will come a time when I'm unselfconsciously who I am on both sides of the border, a Muslim at home at Eric and Lauren's and that earnest American fitting in with the Muslims. *Odysseus will come, within this very cycle of the moon: between the waning and waxing time, he will come home…*

ॐ

I've never worked with Bethany before, but I liked her gentle manners and wide smile whenever we met at midwifery gatherings. Whispering now, I give her a rundown of the day.

"She's been having contractions since about two a.m. They called me to come at 10:15. She's been eating and hydrating well between contractions. Baby sounds great. She really wants to get into the tub, but I wanted her to wait until you got here. The contractions are coming every three to four minutes now. Let me show you my setup so you are familiar with it before the birth."

"Okay, but first I'd like to just sit here and feel out the birth energy, to ground myself in the space," she says as she drags a rocking chair to the bay windows. Sitting in the late afternoon light, backlit by the sun, her curly hair forms a halo around her. With closed eyes and a peaceful countenance, she rocks to the rhythm of Lauren's contractions, increasing her rocking as the peak of the contraction approaches and slowing down as it melts away. From a glance she is the quintessential midwife, calm, confident, and hands off.

But I'm baffled. Transition is a time of labor requiring the focused attention of the birth team, but Bethany just stays put, rocking and rocking. I continue taking notes, staying nearby, listening to baby every fifteen minutes with a Doppler, and charting. Maybe it's because I'm fasting, but I'm irritated. What's the point of another midwife rocking away and grounding into the space? I'm suddenly very self-conscious, the awkward Muslim midwife unsure of how to navigate this terrain. Am I not New Age-y enough? How long is it going to take her to ground into the birth space? If I never do this, does it mean I am "ungrounded" at births?

·

Here they are again, the chorus of my insecurities ascending with the intensity of the labor.

"AAAAAAAAAAAOOOOOOOOOOOOPPPPEEN!" I don't have time to think any longer. Lauren is barreling straight for the tub, no longer waiting for anyone's approval.

"Let me quickly check the temperature first, we have to make sure it's not too hot or cold!" I say as I grab the floating duckie thermometer. It's a perfect 99 degrees. "Get in. It's all yours."

"Thank God!" Lauren exclaims as she peels off her shirt and sinks beneath the water. Eric runs upstairs to get his swim trunks on.

Bethany, finally grounded into the birthing space, comes to squat by the edge of the pool.

"Lauren, you're doing amazing. You are strong and powerful. You are going to birth this baby very soon," she says with full eye contact and a breathy voice.

I wonder if it took her all that time in the rocking chair to come to that realization.

Reaching my hand into the tub, I listen to the baby's heart tones, and I see Lauren, heartened by Bethany's words, gaze into her eyes, maintaining eye contact as the next contraction squeezes her uterus. To be able to hear the heart tones, I must lean way over the birth tub, through two feet of water. When I arise from that feat, the front of my hijab is soaking wet. I wring it out into the birth tub and muster a wan smile.

*Odysseus, you think of going home as honey-sweet, but gods will make it bitter.*

Soon, any irritation or hunger or thirst is erased, as the princess is crowning, occupying all my senses and attention. Lauren's eyes open wide as her mammalian instincts awaken, and she realizes without reasoning or explanation from her birth team what is about to happen.

"AAAAARRRRNNNNNNNNNN!!" Lauren lets out a mammoth roar. I look down and there beneath the water, strands of hair sway gently like sea kelp. The head is out.

"One more push. You're nearly there, the head is out, but you still must push out the body. Slow your breath and wait for the next contraction," I tell her.

The baby's eyes are closed. Floating in the body-temperature water in a state of pure consciousness, it doesn't know it's been born. But we do. Eric is wiping away salty tears. I toss Bethany one of the baby blankets.

I'm elbow deep in the pool now, occupying the expectant space between baby is here, but not. I close my eyes and my hunger comes roaring back to me, catching me off guard.

*The belly is just like a whining dog;*
*It begs and forces one to notice it,*
*Despite exhaustion or the depths of sorrow.*

I look over at Bethany, who, with her beatific smile directed right at me, conveys a trust in birth beyond anything I feel I have. My mask is asunder, and my underlying fears and insecurities feel like they are floating from my head in thought bubbles.

Bethany, her backlit hair still appearing as a golden aura, is serene with the miracle before her. She looks like she belongs here.

"Look at that baby, beautiful…," she mutters and smiles toward Lauren.

My gloved hands are crossed; droplets fall from the wrist opening into the water, waiting and wondering.

Has this past decade removed me from the mannerisms and unspoken cultural currency of the other women in my community? It feels like my home will forever be this liminal space of the new moon before the clouds part, the two weeks before conception folded into the timetable of a yet-to-form embryo, of the space between contractions, of the head before the heart.

This birth tub, hundreds of times bigger than Lauren's womb, is now miraculously, nearly one soul bigger. One soul entered the tub, but two will emerge, one with a softened uterus and arms full of a newborn. Neither I, nor anyone in this steamy dining room, is in control of the outcome of the impending moment of birth. And with that thought, I am comforted. The expectant spaces between, the miles from home, shrink into the daily gestures of holy grandeur.

Lauren wordlessly looks each one of us in the eye before going inward one last time for the final push. As she does, I guide out shoulders, spine, hips, and feet, and deliver a screaming wet baby through the water's surface to the gravity of Lauren's chest.

"Oh my *God*! We did it!! Our baby is here, Eric!"

"You're a rock star, babe," Eric says with that partly cloudy face of new fathers, a lustrous smile through eyes brimming. He gazes adoringly at the baby in his wife's arms.

"She's beautiful. Just look at her little rosebud mouth. I'm so proud of you!" I say as I grab a stray cup to pour warm water right over the blanket covering baby, in order to keep the half of baby peeking out of the water as warm as the legs kicking beneath the water like a tadpole's tail exploring its pond.

Bethany is looking on with a preternatural calm from her perch near Lauren's shoulder. Everyone is now waiting for the placenta, while I'm waiting for a tall glass of water. The birth tub has made the room hot and steamy. My mouth is parched.

"Let me know when you feel a cramp. There is still a placenta," I instruct Lauren. Baby, wrapped securely in her mother's arms, is still connected to the umbilical cord. Bethany takes over the job of pouring water on baby to keep her warm, and for the next quarter of an hour, that is the only sound we hear, a gentle whoosh of water followed by silence.

Lauren begins to moan, signaling the placenta's arrival. I gently provide traction on the umbilical cord. Bethany grabs the placenta bowl, a medium-size mixing bowl I include in the birth supply list. I feel the cord lengthen and, soon, the tension of a placenta at the other end, and then plop, out it comes, membranes and all into the mixing bowl.

"That feels so good!" Lauren exclaims. She is, officially, no longer pregnant.

"Doesn't it? Let's check and see if the cord is done pulsing, if so, let's cut the cord and hand baby to dad so we can get you dried off and out of the birth tub."

Lauren agrees and I hand Bethany the placenta bowl. Peeling back the layers of baby blanket to find the cord, I am surprised to discover a little penis!

"Lauren! It's a boy!"

"*What?*" she throws the blanket off and lifts the baby up to verify. "What the hell? Eric, look at that!! It's a *boy!*"

Eric is astonished. Lauren and I cannot stop laughing.

ॐ

The sun's rays are long in the sky as I'm packing my things and tucking Lauren in. Bethany is winding the umbilical cord into a spiral, explaining how she will dry this and turn it into a teething toy for the baby. She takes the placenta home to turn into capsules for Lauren to ingest daily during the postpartum weeks. They are both very excited over these things.

I will never be that midwife. I will not rock my way into the energetics of a birth room, nor wind umbilical cords into spirals. But neither am I destined to be the midwife defined only by difference. Just like the fast can transcend the lack of food, I can transcend the discomfort of my identity. I can belong to both sides of myself without any water beneath.

Lauren smiles at me from beneath her cozy covers. "That was amazing. Thank you, Shannon. And now we can throw out all of that pink crap!"

ॐ

*After many years*
*Of agony and absence from one's home,*
*A person can begin enjoying grief*

I'm unsure whether I would recognize home anymore or, like Odysseus coming home disguised in the garb of a bent and aged man, whether it would recognize me. As with Odysseus's journey home, each birth I attend presents a journey within a journey, an exhuming of the insecurities and uncertainties of this unorthodox path I have chosen—a contraction that requires the softening and surrender modeled by a mother in labor—and a resolution that brings me closer.

The mystery of the path, of the calendar, of when a woman will deliver her baby, can link us back to our origins. Shaykh Hamza identifies the reason of finding a high point and going to sight the moon each lunar cycle:

Connecting people with the natural phenomenon in our selves and on the horizon—which is where we must look

178

every month for the new moon—is a central aim and purpose of the religion itself.

Birth, in all its unknowns, has served this purpose for me. While it can shake my confidence in the outward manifestations of fitting in that my faith delineates for me, internally it serves to strengthen my certainty in the Divine, Who without aid, causes Ramadan to begin, causes a mother to bear her pregnancy for two weeks and two days past the calculated time, and causes a girl, her sex decreed by the unblinking eye of an ultrasound, to in truth be a boy.

His parents, however, stuck to the name Juniper.

Lauren would go on to deliver one more baby with me, also in Ramadan, and also two weeks and two days past her due date. That time they skipped the ultrasound. She once again labored in the tub, but so much quieter this time that while I was upstairs sneaking in a hurried pre-dawn meal before the day of fasting began, I nearly missed the birth.

*Soon Dawn was born, her fingers bright with roses.*

"Shannon, stop eating and get down here!" cried Lauren seconds before she delivered yet another soul into the warm waters of a birth tub.

I ran down the stairs to find her pulling her baby once again from the water's surface, his cry singular in the rising day.

In his book, Shaykh Hamza explores the meaning of the word both for the sighting of the new moon and for birth: "Birth (*ih-lal*) can also refer to the cry one makes upon sighting the crescent, which was later used metaphorically to refer to a baby's cry upon being born."

Birth is sometimes like that, hurried and wild, like the moon that asserts itself above the descending sun.

# CHAPTER 10

*Peace—a word from a merciful Lord.*

—Qur'an 36:58

The gray area of when labor starts is rarely heralded by a neat "five minutes apart, lasting one minute, for at least one hour," otherwise known as 511, but shhh, don't tell my midwifery clients. As a midwife, I can recognize labor's approach in the puffed faces of my beautiful mothers, their mental desperation and physical distress at a state that is starting to feel timeless. As a mother, I recognize it in myself when I start to burn things in the kitchen consistently, each meal somehow derailed, for days. My mind is incredibly present, but not. It is the outward manifestation of the internal contradiction—in the invariable discomforts of late pregnancy, I find myself yearning for escape though the rhythmic pain of contractions.

I have just felt three contractions in a half hour. They squeeze my middle, forcing me to sway my hips and breathe. The baby even pauses its passes at my ribs, seeming to wonder at the new sensations too. I call my husband at work, wanting him to be on alert. The kitchen is inside out with half-finished projects, date balls needing to be rolled and dipped in coconut, salsa needing to be chopped and bottled, milk cooling for yogurt, beans bubbling for tonight's enchiladas, and a sink full of the evidence. It's at least an hour or two of work, and my labors rarely last that long. My mind is swimming between before and after. Now, I'm a pregnant mother preparing her family for her postpartum rest. After, I'm on the other side of this great battle called labor.

I've been advised by many to listen to the Chapter of Mary in the Qur'an during labor. It is what fits right now. I plug my phone into the speakers. "Kaf. Ha. Ya. Ayn. Sad" rings out of the portable speakers and reverberates through my entire being on such a physical level that I grab the counter's edge and sink down to the kitchen floor. The soothing words and rhythm continue to wash over me, melding the before and after of this fragile expectant mother. I am reminded that if I die in childbirth, I am a martyr, receiving the same spiritual status as one who dies in the way of God. I weep for a forgiveness I didn't know needed forgiving. It feels like the shedding of a self, one that needs to yield in order for a momentous event to occur.

Salek overhears the weeping and asks, "Are you having contractions?" Yes, I answer him, noting mentally, that no, I haven't felt them since I called my husband half an hour ago, but there is no other explanation for my unraveling in the kitchen, so I do what most mothers do and opt for expediency. I hear him tell his sister that the baby is coming. I am once again grounded by my sweet children. The enchiladas need to be rolled. I hit "Translate" on the Qur'an app on my phone. The verse playing at that moment answers my misgivings, "So eat and drink and be contented." My heart swells with belief, and I am back on the staircase weeping. Allah is *al-Hayy*, the Living, and I am not alone in this undertaking. The kitchen can wait, I finish listening to the chapter before resuming my work. I imagine that this is what a soldier feels like before battle, humbled ego and steadied heart.

Reflecting now on my three labors, I can etch out some individual patterns: not only does my water break before my labors, but it does so at the beginning of the morning prayer. It's an odd pattern, but I like it.

I'm lying in bed as my husband rouses himself for *fajr*, the dawn prayer, when a contraction hits me so hard, I reach out for his arm. And then with a great release, I feel the soothing warmth of amniotic fluid, a message from the other side, my baby's habitat for the past nine months revealed. Instantly, I am shivering and moaning through contractions. It's odd to be a midwife and a mother in labor, with the contrast between the head and the heart somehow more distinct. I'm noting from a distant place in my head that I am in transition. I tell my husband to call the midwife, but tell her not to come, the heart is wanting privacy. I am playing that mind game that mothers in labor play. We tell ourselves that this is only the beginning in order to have mental stamina for the end, and in some ways, labor really is only the beginning.

The morning prayers are said, and we are descending the staircase so that these moans of "Ooooopppppeeennn" do not wake the sleeping children. By the time we make it to our living room, the birth room, I am nauseous and hot. I want a wet washcloth, and a woman's knowing touch. My beloved Judy now lives less than a mile away. "Call her," I tell my devoted husband, who is fumbling with the birth tub pump. She answers and says, "I'm already on my way"—did we think she was waiting for another call? Midwives, the good ones, capture that difficult place between knowing and unknowing with such skill and wit.

I am sending each contraction into circles of movement, from hips to cervix. I can't imagine not circling my hips. "Ya Latif, O Gentle One," I mutter, weaving this sentiment into these circles. I am connected to my Muslim sisters from Afghanistan to Senegal, who have uttered this divine name through their contractions for centuries. They become my companions through these giant, urgent waves. I can do this too.

The birth tub is inflated but dry as I am feeling the first urges to push. There is no time to fill it. I have never done this without the tub, and I am nervous. How do I push outside of water? The answer soon becomes clear: you just do. Twenty minutes later, my nine pound, ten ounce baby boy is born. We name him Ya Sin, a name without direct meaning, yet laden with divine mysteries and meanings—two letters to remind us that God doesn't leave even the smallest of minutiae, the letters that make up a word, bereft of significance. It is what I felt throughout this pregnancy and the earliest twinges of labor, a knowing beneath the surface that if trusted and sought will open up worlds of understanding.

# CHAPTER 11

*It is essential to realize that we cannot reach the inner mean-*
*ing of the Quran until we ourselves have penetrated into the*
*deeper dimensions of our being and also by the grace of*
*Heaven.*

—Seyyed Hossein Nasr, *Ideals and Realities of Islam*

Beside their husband, between the two wives, sits a steaming bowl of barley and broth. The one who made it, the second wife, begs the first wife to try some of her cooking. When the first wife defers, the second one says playfully, "If you don't eat some of this food, I'll wipe it on your face!" The first still refuses, and so the second wife makes good on her offer and wipes some of the barley across her cheek. Their husband, bemused, then encourages his older, perhaps less mirthful, first wife, to retaliate. "What are you waiting for?" he goads. "Smear her face too!"

In another story, that same second wife has heard rumors of the beauty of the newest wife. Unable to contain herself, she walks, disguised in a full veil, to the reception where the unveiled bride's beauty can be inspected. The husband, despite the veil, recognizes his second wife and follows her outside, "How did you find her, O Aisha?" Aisha, the second wife, doesn't let her jealousy peek through her veil and shrugs it off, replying non-chalantly that this one is no different than any other woman of her tribe.

One time their husband is gifted a black onyx necklace and, in the company of his wives, says, "I shall give this unto the one I love best of all." The shifting of their robes along with the whispered conjectures that it will go to the presumed favorite, the second wife, fills the expectant air. Their husband then looks around the room, pausing at each one of them, keeping them in suspense until his eyes alight on his little granddaughter Umamah, and he calls her to him and clasps the necklace around her dainty neck.

Their husband is no ordinary husband, but the Prophet Muhammad ﷺ, and these are no ordinary women. Known collectively as the Mothers of the Believers, the wives of the Prophet Muhammad are among the most relatable people in the prophetic biography. Muslims have preserved stories of one wife's bald jealousy over another's supposed beauty while yet another wife comforts away the panicked state wrought by that envy; of one wife's wise counsel to her husband who needed to appease a community seething at being denied their rights to make the pilgrimage to Mecca; of how the wives could conspire against one another but also provide each other with a deep connection and sisterhood during times of loss and times of plenty. When pushed to their limits, these women always chose God and His Messenger.

The wives of the Prophet modeled a deep humanity, an embodied existence that also manifested in ways unique to each of them. Khadija, the only wife of the Prophet for 25 years, steady, wise, and maternal. Sawda, the one he married after his first wife's death, tall, reserved, loving. Aisha, the beloved redhead with a brilliant intellect, a logical mind, an outspoken lover of poetry. Zaynab, a renowned beauty and talented artisan of leather goods with a profound bent to charity. They weren't following a template of how a Muslim woman should behave; they were the first generation of Muslims, the light of guidance still in their midst, a light that didn't dim their own individual characteristics, each a prism with her own luster and glimmer.

For me, without the benefit of cultural intimacy, the notion of a Muslim woman often seems to hold less room for individual difference. When in gatherings, I was left with the feeling that some of these women must float through their days, buoyant with pious devotion, for they never had much to share when asked how they were doing—*alhamdulillah*, "praise God," was often as far as I would get before we each looked around awkwardly searching for something to say. Where was Aisha with the lines of memorized poetry to lift our spirits and awaken our minds? Or Zaynab with her eye for artistry and beauty? While these women may have felt at ease with one another, I often felt heavy and incompatible, searching for connection. There was a uniformity to their speech, dress, and interests I couldn't quite decipher. Everyone seemed to shine with the same wattage, and the more time I spent in the confines of a community connected by religion but not culture, the more I struggled to raise or lower my own dimmer accordingly.

When I was learning about Islam I picked up a book off the bottom shelf in a St. Louis bookstore called *Ideals and Realities of Islam* by the American Iranian scholar Seyyed Hossein Nasr—the title itself has given me much solace over the years. The Mothers of the Believers were the ideal, but the reality is often the space between the *alhamdulillah* and the pith of the real emotional answer embedded therein.

ଚ୍ଚ

It's August in the Bay Area; the fog has lifted and the bright days of summer have finally commenced. I have two first-time moms due, but each of them is already a family of three; in one month I am caring for two polygamous families. Rather than witnessing food fights and a husband's playful teasing, I am struggling to see the domestic joy in these homes.

In one family, the second wife is pregnant. One day her co-wife calls me to deliver the news, which she stutters out after I promise I won't judge her for what she's about to tell me. "Shannon, well, okay, I'm calling because, I need to tell you, Layla is my husband's second wife."

I don't want to pause for too long, yet neither do I want to do what I just reassured her I wouldn't do and am now doing—judging. "I wondered if that wasn't the case. I couldn't make out what your relationship with her was. And how is that for you? You are okay with everything? Does she live with you?"

"Yes. SubhanAllah, Shannon, Allah put it in my heart that I don't have any problem with her and in fact, I love her. My kids though, they do have a problem. Especially the older ones who now understand that marriage entails sex. Once they understood that, they cannot forgive their father for doing this to their mother. It is very hard for them, and that is what makes it hard for me, not Layla or my husband."

From the outside it looks like every Orientalist trope about polygamy in Islam, that once childbearing and time wear down the first wife, the man can snag a fresh, pretty wife and start all over again. Layla comes to each prenatal with her eyeliner freshly applied, her hijab in the latest style atop high heels and a Coach purse, while the first wife bares a face without a dot of makeup and dons a long dark polyester abaya, a shadow to the second's dazzle.

In the other family, the first wife is pregnant. When I visit her suburban home after an unplanned cesarean section, she admits that the day after the birth, her husband resumed his visits to the second wife. Every other night, Asma, while recovering from a major surgery, found herself alone with a newborn who wasn't breastfeeding well, causing her intense nipple pain.

"The nights are so hard. I just need someone to change a diaper so I can go back to sleep for a little bit." She bursts into tears at the admission.

The realities of polygamy in the twenty-first century manifest so much differently from the ideals lived a millennium and a half earlier.

∞

"Hello? Is this Shannon? Shannon! I can't believe I'm talking to you. Sydney is a friend of mine, and she gave me your contact information. I read your blog and just love-love-love it. Can you be my midwife?"

"Sure!" I laugh. "Do you have any questions about home birth or midwifery first?"

"Well, I have recently arrived from Cairo and now I am pregnant. I don't know much about home birth or midwives other than from your blog and Sydney, but I'm sure that's what I want. The only thing is my family, they are not going to like this idea of home birth, but since they are all in Egypt, let's see!" Her accent sounds more French than Arab, but the charm is universal. We arrange to meet at her apartment in a little over a week.

By now, I have a template in my head for Muslims from overseas who desire a home birth: generally heavy on the Islam, a *niqab* and a husband who won't make eye contact. They own very few books outside of gilded religious texts. I'm usually referred to as "sister." Without a common culture, Islam becomes what binds and connects us. Unable to stretch into other areas of shared relevance, our bond, though sincere, ends at sisters in faith. Often I come home with a plate of homemade baklava or *gulab jamon*, the syrupy deserts cloying to my palate, more accustomed to my grandmother's gingersnap cookies.

Their apartment is in West Oakland, a gritty part of the city across the highway from downtown's skyscrapers. Like every other part of Oakland, West Oakland is quickly gentrifying. I buzz their apartment but no one answers, so I sit on the stoop and survey the neighborhood; a homeless man pushes a cart filled with dirty blankets and rattling empty cans down the sidewalk toward the liquor store. He's not too steady on his feet and stops often to catch his breath. I click my car's lock key just to be sure. There is a constant din from the bordering highway. The graffiti pops beneath the strength of the sunlight. The choice of this neighborhood for these newly landed immigrants piques my interest.

My phone buzzes with a text from Seema. "We are almost there. Sooooo sorry. I am on the lookout for an antique sewing machine, and I had to come to the flea market to look for one." I look toward the Oakland skyline and mentally rearrange my idea of "Arab immigrant."

ॐ

I'm not expecting Seema. There is no preparing for brilliance; you simply meet it and try not to squint.

"Shaannoon! There you are. I hope you weren't waiting long. Isn't it a gorgeous day?" Seema turns the corner, her warm grin and sparkling wideset eyes topped with a wrapped floral turban. As promised, she is lugging an antique sewing machine.

Instantly, she takes up a sizeable piece of land in my heart.

From the outside, her home is all barred windows and a neglected lawn, but Seema has turned the small one bedroom into a cozy and hip den. West African mudcloth hangs on the wall, Ikea beds have been turned into lavish sofas, and pegboards hang in the kitchen and living room, storing all kinds of unexpected utensils and displaying her latest art inspiration.

"Can I get you some tea? Nuts? Lamb stew? I make really good lamb stew." Amir, Seema's husband, lean and swift, is poking through the cupboards as he speaks.

"I'll take some tea, thank you."

"Are you sure, no lamb stew? I just have to defrost the lamb and cut the vegetables. Then I will put it in the slow cooker for a few hours. The best lamb stew you ever had!" His earnest face awaits an answer.

"Amir! He's joking! Can you make her some tea, please? And I'll take a cup too, of the red raspberry leaf tea. I'm so excited you are here. Where do we start?"

"Well, do you have any questions or concerns about home birth?" I'm treading carefully, as I'm not sure what to make of them. They could be any Oakland couple having a home birth, yet they've only been in California nine months. As far as I know, home birth is not a popular option for Cairene women, and in my experience, women who come from, or even whose mothers come from, countries with high maternal and infant mortality rates carry an almost irrational fear of birth, an inherited terror of losing one's life in the birthing process. Yet, here is Seema, planning a home birth with a midwife she has just met.

"Yes, I mean I have questions, but I just really want to have my baby at home. I've been reading your blog and watching YouTube videos, and it all seems so spiritual and magical. I'm sort of like you, Shannon, I'm like a convert." Seema tells me she wasn't always a practicing Muslim and that she was swept up in the excitement of the Arab Spring. "At first we were all excited, but when things didn't change, I was depressed." Much like me, she discovered Muslim scholars who understood the West. "I found hope and solace in the way they presented Islam."

"But your family is Muslim, so they must be happy?"

"Well, it's different there. We come from the upper class, and in Egypt, the lower class are the religious ones. My mother-in-law told me I look like the housekeeper with my hijab on."

"Oh," I say lamely, trying to hide my surprise. "You are like a convert then! Why don't I give you my spiel about home birth; what happens in an emergency, what the care looks like, and where we go from here? You can ask me any questions after that."

"I will just be over here working on your stew!" Amir shouts from the kitchen.

"Amir, can we have our teas already?" laughs Seema.

℘

Sometimes when I meet other Muslims, it's as if we are crossing the same border but going in different directions. One of us is leaving and the other, entering. There is a faint recognition, but also a confusion—why are you leaving all that I am entering?

It could seem like the ones leaving their Islamic faith in the background have all the creativity, spark, and drive, while the ones whose faith stays in the foreground are sober and technical.

The further I got from my own origins and natal creativity, the more I felt the need to fit into my chosen faith community, over time adopting the customs and dress, shaving the round peg of my personality more and more to fit into the square hole of the community I saw around me, but trailing wood shavings like a Hansel in case I ever needed to find my way home.

Americans and the Muslims I often meet exist on two opposite ends of divorced traditions. In his book *The Devil Knows Latin*, E. Christian Kopff argues that American society, cut off from its Greek and Latin roots, exists in a perpetual state of "simple innovation." He explains, "Creativity is possible only as the final stage in a long, rigorous absorption of the teachings and discoveries of the past."

Americans today are constantly striving to create anew, without looking upstream to see how the water tables are doing or even where they originate. There is a feebleness to our creative output—shallow roots leaving us prone to rot.

Devout Muslims in America, on the other hand, know that their only success lies in turning back to their rooted center, the abundant spring of the Qur'an and the life of the Prophet and his companions. Like Americans, they, however, are often linguistically cut off from the tradition, able to recite Arabic as a sacred language, yet not fluent enough to study its texts. Therefore, Muslims, rather than forging ahead with a creativity blind to its origins, carefully preserve what has been so lovingly entrusted to them, the practice and implementation of a faith across time and space. What may seem stuffy to me is in fact generated from a place of awe and humility, the weight of a tradition that Americans have hardly borne.

In a way, Seema linked arms with me and turned me back toward the lands from which I was absconding, her appreciation for culture and creativity refreshing, while showing me that the fields of Islam could grow more than one kind of crop—Islam was not a monoculture. She had an immediate discomfort with the inordinate number of *insha'Allah*s and *masha'Allah*s peppered into American Muslim dialogues, balancing her religion with more grace and ease, and less show and artifice. My Islam seemed clunky, less subtle than hers. Her ability to infuse the Islam handed down to her with the kaleidoscope of Western creativity allowed the light of her diamond to scatter in a prism of colors, inviting me to do the same.

છ

"Let's talk about the stages of labor. For a first-time mom, the average labor lasts 20 hours. On the early side of those 20 hours, you will either want to go back to sleep, or find a project to distract yourself," I explained. In preparing first-time moms for labor, I have learned to be comforted by expressions of fear and anxiety; the acknowledgment of the steep path ahead fosters a humility and engenders a focused preparation in mothers, stockpiling electrolytes and mental affirmations for the ascent.

The ones who don't display fear or anxiety signal a lack of understanding of the determination and commitment needed to withstand labor's throes. A midwife must prepare the mother as fathers once prepared sons for battle, not the battles of today, the push-button bombs and drones, but the hand-to-hand combat of the past, where you could smell your foe's sweat, and the mission of the fight fostered courage and focus. A midwife must prepare the first-time mother delicately, inculcating bravery without scaring her.

"Shannon, I am an African woman; I can handle birth," Seema replies.

Laughing at her bravado, I say, "Right, I don't remember childbirth classes in Senegal, come to think of it."

When I was pregnant with Fatimah, a friend of mine had traveled to the Hadramaut Valley in Yemen, a richly spiritual place rooted in Sufism and Islamic tradition. With a high fertility rate, pregnancy and labor are frequent topics of conversation among the women there.

She related that in Yemen pregnant women would write out the Qur'anic chapter called The Smoke in miniscule script, roll it up into a miniature scroll, and place it in a locket under strict instruction not to wear it until birth commenced.

"Look out," she had warned, "it works really quickly. It makes the labor smooth and swift."

*Like smoke,* I thought, sticking it in my midwife toolbox. I'd known midwives who swore by stranger things to facilitate labor; showers, shots of espresso, vitamin B12 shots, intimacy with a partner between contractions! Working alone, often in the middle of the night, makes for resourceful midwives. At my next visit with Seema, I suggested the tiny scroll was worth a try. By our following visit, true to form, Seema had a bespoke necklace, the Qur'anic verse printed out and folded within. We are an ageless partnership, the midwife offering medicine from our shared faith, and the mother, willing to rely and rest on the force of that.

ॐ

"Shannon, these contractions are no joke." Amir's voice is edged with concern. "We have gone for a walk, and taken a shower, and they just keep coming. Seema is doing well, but it's getting hard for her."

"Why don't you have her lay down on her left side. Call me in an hour." This is my standard advice to first-time parents, who often mistake the earliest signs of labor for active labor. She has only been at it an hour or two, and her contractions are about six minutes apart. I figure I have time to rest for at least that long before having to head over.

In exactly an hour, Amir is again on the other end of the line. "Shannon, now they are very close together, and she is saying she can't do it."

"Okay, let me listen to her for a contraction or two." I settle beneath my blankets, thinking I will be able to enjoy their warmth again as soon as we hang up, but the minute I hear Seema's next contraction, insistent and guttural, I am sitting straight up in bed, the adrenaline rushing through my muscles.

"I'm heading over now. These sound like strong contractions." I don't even finish my sentence before she has another one. I shiver into the clothes I had set out and rouse my husband to help transport my birth bags into the car.

I'm still baffled by how quickly her labor is progressing. *I should know by now to expect the unexpected with this one,* I tell myself.

Some women pace in labor; Seema is stalking. She crosses the length of her apartment as if looking for prey. The ever-present spark has transformed into a fire, a wildfire wanting to engulf these contractions. To say she does not like labor is an understatement; she despises it. Any magical ideas she had about a serene labor were gone hours ago.

"Shannon, this is ridiculous. It is so hard and soooo pain-oooooohhhhhhhhhh …" Seema is thrust into the eye of the storm with this contraction, bending at the waist. I begin the ritual of unpacking the birth supplies by flashlight, for besides the streetlight, there is no other light on in the apartment, as if dusk fell and they were so consumed by the contractions, they didn't notice the lights weren't on.

"You're doing amazing! You're going to meet your baby so soon. Would you like to know how far along you are? We don't have to, but we can check and see how many centimeters your cervix has opened." I look to her and Amir, who are both enthusiastically nodding; they've been in the dark long enough.

As we are walking to the bedroom, that's when I notice it—the necklace with the Qur'anic verse wound into the locket dangling from her neck.

&

They fell in love during the heady time of the Arab Spring in Egypt. After overthrowing a dictator, working to solve the undeniable equation of millions minus one dictator equals freedom, anything was possible. Yet, the labor is proving harder than reversing nearly thirty years of autocracy.

"Seema! Amir! Your baby is almost here! You are seven centimeters! Let me call the other midwife."

Amir, I must remember, is not the hipster dad from Oakland who has watched all the home birth videos and taken all the childbirth education classes; a part of him is still an Egyptian man. He looks at me like I've just told him aliens have landed beneath the streetlight. "It's here? Can, can I see?"

"Well, it's not here, here, but it's very close. There's a small amount of cervix left, but soon, Amir, soon." He looks visibly relieved, but also a little frazzled. Fatherhood hasn't given him much lead time.

"I want to get out of this position!!" Seema roars back to life, and as the next contraction seizes her, she flips to her hands and knees as gracefully as a rabbit leaps a garden fence.

I'm trying my best to protect the mattress from getting soiled, shoving clean chux pads underneath her and around her.

Between contractions, I rest my hand on her lower back, giving her a sense of grounding. *You're here on the bed, beneath my hand. You're still a body; here is your spine.* It can be so easy at this point in labor for a mother to spin off and disconnect from her body, to focus only on the immense pressure sensations, that they can almost overwhelm her. Eye contact and a grounding touch often do the trick. I'm not sure if it's working for Seema.

"UUUNNHH! I'm pushing!" Seema shouts, her voice almost edged with anger at the affront.

"That's fine," I say, "go ahead." Right then the front door buzzes; the assist midwife has just arrived. Amir is torn—should he stay or go let the midwife in? "Can you run quickly and let her in?" I ask, once again underestimating the time it will take to push this baby out and how swiftly Amir moves.

It all happens in a flash—Amir runs in, followed closely by the other midwife, when the head pops out followed by the rest of the squat body, and it's over. The primal chaos gives way to a surreal stillness. The armor falls away, the weapons are laid down, the anger of the battle is replaced by a soft and hard-earned sense of peace. He is here. The battle has been won.

Amir holds his son, the cord still attached, as we help unwind baby and flip Seema to her back. Dad hands baby to mom, who nestles him immediately by her side, and I stand at the end of the bed, waiting for that jubilant exhale, that outpouring of emotion that often accompanies births, but there is none. They are simply together, the arithmetic of birth, plus one, just now adding up.

ℰℴ

When I visit Seema the next day, her mother has arrived from Egypt. It is now clear to see that Seema is the splendor reflected—Lamis is an impeccably dressed queen with elegant manners, along with an old-world warmth that instantly puts one at ease. If she had any misgivings about the home birth, she is too gracious to say so.

"Good job, Shannon! You did a wonderful job with Seema and Haroon." She is holding her grandson, Haroon, and ushering me to sit in the living room.

"Seema did all the hard work," I say.

"Hey, didn't you see how quickly I ran down the stairs, let the other midwife in, and made it back in time for the birth? That was hard work too! I actually feel a little sore from that sprint," Amir jokes.

"Where is Seema? I'll do a quick checkup with mom and baby, and then I'll leave you all to visit."

It's always my goal to return the next day to make sure mothers are in bed resting well. Seema was doing just that. The Saturday bustle of Oakland was alive and well outside, while inside the apartment, the slow, still pace of life with a newborn reigned.

Seema smiles at me sheepishly, "Shannon, that was not what I expected! I didn't think it would be so hard. I feel like this is God's way of showing me my arrogance or something, like I thought I was a 'strong African woman,' but those contractions were stronger than me! The minute I put on that necklace with Surah Dukhan, it just sped ahead."

"Why did you put that on right away? Remember, I told you to wait until we confirmed that active labor had started? Aha! It's all making sense now," I tease her.

"Yeah, that really works! I don't know." Seema bites her bottom lip, struggling to find the words. "I feel kind of traumatized by the labor. It was so, so hard, not at all 'magical' or even spiritual. It felt violent. I totally understand women who get epidurals. I would have gotten an epidural if I had been in the hospital. I would have paid lots of money to make the contractions stop!"

She tenderly adjusts herself into a sitting position, her gorgeous face belying a vulnerability and sadness I hadn't seen before. The eagerness and confidence are now replaced with an uncertainty and traces of disappointment. "I don't feel anything like a birth high. I was expecting to feel so bonded to him and to fall instantly in love."

Amir has been sitting on the edge of the bed. "Yeah, at first, I didn't have those feelings of 'this is the best thing to ever happen to me.' I just felt like, 'Oh, he's here.' And also, I didn't think the labor would be that hard for her!"

It is hard not to feel defensive, because I so want my clients to come away from home birth empowered by their experience, not traumatized by it. But I had to admit, there is an edge of viciousness to contractions that can be shocking to comprehend in the days following. After Salek was born, I remember being taken aback at my own reflection, not by the under-eye puffiness and dark circles caused by the sleep deprivation, but by the fact that my reflection was, for the most part, unchanged. I felt so altered by the experience of birth, that I wondered if a part of me hadn't been buried with the placenta. I thought, *This is a taste of death.* I felt extinguished.

Yet perhaps this relinquishing is the gift of birth, the fertile land after a fire, offering women a renewal. The ideals and realities of a natural birth are the entropy of birth yielding a new internal order.

After taking a few moments to ponder, all I can say is, "I'm so sorry that you feel that way. Give it a few days; you might feel better. But you don't have to love it either. I never met a woman who said, 'If I could just have one more contraction.'"

"I guess I'm not that strong African woman!" laughs Seema.

Lamis brings in a fussy Haroon, whom I help attach to his mother's breast and wonder how different the outer experience can be from the inner experience. Perhaps where there's smoke, there's not always fire.

§

I know the ending to this story: the birth trauma, with time, healed. Seema went on to have another fist-pumping adrenaline rush of a birth. This time, however, Lamis, her mother, was there for all of it: holding Seema's hand and watching gracefully from the bedside as her daughter met the steepness of the challenge with strong quads and measured breath. Seema's daughter was born with less fire and more water; there was not a dry eye in the room.

In time I would see the polygamous families meld into a more coherent version of family. In the extra room the women alternately occupied on their nights away from their husband, the first wife supported the second wife throughout the labor, massaging her shoulders, speaking gentle, encouraging words, and, when it was time for the birth, even calling their husband into the room to welcome their newest family member.

In the other family, I would see the baby as a toddler, kept safe by the second wife from wandering outside the mosque onto the busy Oakland streets, while the first wife was able to finish a meal and relax with her friends without the distraction of her son. Their realities resembling more of the ideals.

§

Seema and Amir had decided to leave Egypt soon after the ousting of Hosni Mubarak, for they found it soul crushing to wander the same streets that months before had energized their hopes for the country, now in the hands of another autocrat. The ideals of the heady days of revolution were replaced by unbending political realities.

One of the common reasons women experience birth trauma is that providers fail to convey a picture of the road ahead. Maybe with more birth education from myself, Seema's nervous system would have been better prepared for the rigors of contractions:

less emphasis on the ideals and more on the realities of the squeeze of uterine muscles. Yet without the exertions of labor, there is no momentous alteration in a woman—motherhood loses some of its depth.

By placing my hopes of acceptance and contentment in a community that itself was so fragmented and embryonic, I was confusing the shallows for the depths. I needed to reorient my longing to God, the immutable force I had sought before and after my conversion, without the gnawing need to belong so neatly within a broader community. For so long now, identity had replaced seeking. The brittleness of that splintered into a million dazzling shards of a cracked mirror, and I was trying to compile a version of myself in its pieces. My true belonging could only come from God.

But as Rumi says, "Who could be so lucky? Who comes to a lake for water and sees the reflection of the moon?"

# CHAPTER 12

*America needs to understand Islam because this is the one religion that erases from its society the race problem.*

—Malcolm X

It's drizzling. After a long train ride out of Grand Central Station, a confusing drive through the suburban streets of Hartford, New York, with our uber-patient Uber driver, we finally arrive at our destination. The woman at the information desk, pointing out the path on the map, seems uncertain. I wonder if it's because there are few visitors here.

"Do people come to visit him?" I ask.

"Yes," she replies, "nearly every day. It's a long walk. Are you sure you're okay to walk it in this weather?"

With map in hand, we weave our way through the chilly drizzle past the graves of philanthropists, actors, and diplomats, their marble gravestones prominent and upright. My heart pounds with anticipation as I scan the route between the headstones and the highlighted path on the map. I grab Najeeb's hand, and we walk on in expectant silence.

৪১

Earlier that week I had been in Maine for the annual Midwives Association of North America conference. Amid breakout sessions on cannabis in pregnancy, gastrointestinal birth defects, and birthing multiples, I sensed a slow simmer of resentment and identity politics. Birth can be a reflection of culture, and this conference of midwives and birth professionals in 2018 America proved no exception. Even the universal experience of birth is divided by America's defining issue, race.

A quick history lesson: When a campaign led by the American Medical Association abolished midwifery in segregated America, most nonimmigrant white women swiftly integrated into the hospital system, while black women and their midwives chose, whether out of necessity or desire, to stay home to birth their babies, effectively preserving the knowledge and skills of midwifery in America. When anti-establishment white women in the sixties and seventies rediscovered midwifery, the unbroken traditions of birth in the black community went unacknowledged. Now white women, many of them pioneers from midwifery's resurgence, headed the national midwifery organizations and institutions, leaving, according to the narrative unfolding in recent years, women of color, especially black midwives, sidelined and ignored.

At the conference's lobster dinner, things reach a head. By request of the women of color, the organizers separate the midwives by race—the black and indigenous midwives in one room, with the white midwives in another. The entertainment for the evening, an all-female percussion and vocal group, is scheduled to perform, for some unknown reason, only in the room where the white midwives are dining. I am seated next to a kind, mustachioed gentleman with a Midwestern brogue, who shows me how to use the lobster cracker and the small lobster knife to get to the tender meat. We are all wearing plastic bibs. I feel flattened by the state of affairs.

Even if black and brown midwives initiated the separation, it seems backward to racially segregate dinner in 2018. My friend Sydney, also a convert to Islam and a newly licensed midwife in New Jersey, has also been siphoned into the dining room for white midwives. A few years earlier, she and her then husband visited California. Gathered in my living room around a whole grilled fish, a vibrant beet salad, and roast potatoes sat two Cubans, a Pakistani, a Pole, an Irishman, and a Filipino, all of us Muslim—our children mirrored the palette of our evening's dessert, sweet vanilla, salted caramel, and milk chocolate. We couldn't have segregated that dinner if we tried.

Optimistically hoping Sydney, despite her progressive leanings, will resonate with my unease, I ask, "Do you really think this is necessary? It seems divisive to me."

"It's good," she assures me. "They need a safe space to talk amongst themselves. That's the least we could do, to provide them with a safe space." This type of segregation doesn't faze Sydney at all. I can see that her views are more acceptable in today's racial climate, but I'm still uneasy.

I counter, "Aren't midwives the originators of 'safe space'? What hope is there if this small group of nurturing home birth midwives can't get this right? And also, Sydney, do Muslims belong in the 'white' room?"

"Of course, we're white, Shannon. We are racialized, but we are not black." *Racialized*. This wasn't a term yet in my vocabulary. All I could think of was that if Sydney was black or Pakistani, we would be separated by our race, despite our shared religion.

Despite living as a visible religious minority all these years, I had never conceived of myself as entering America's delicate conversation around race. I certainly didn't know I had been racialized. Had my white skin become a shade darker under my hijab? As a grade schooler, I had pored over the nation's history of separate water fountains and segregated schools, appalled that such cruelty was only so recently legislated away. My grandfather told me stories of how black men would step in the gutter to let him pass when he would walk down St. Paul's streets, disturbing my sense of a country from which I had known fairness and decency. To compare my life as a Muslim woman with the lives of African American women in the Jim Crow South or the impoverished ghettos of the north seemed not only disproportionate to but also disrespectful of the real oppression faced by black people in this country. Yet increasingly, I was seeing my fellow Muslims compare Islamophobia to racism, using arguments about marginalization similar to those the black and indigenous midwives were making at the conference. That's what Sydney meant by *racialization*, but even for her, our whiteness superseded our racialized identities, an equation that placed two Muslims in the white dining room among secular, Wiccan, and a sprinkling of Christian midwives.

Caner Dagli, a professor of religious studies at the College of the Holy Cross in Massachusetts, wrote an article in Zaytuna College's journal, *Renovatio*, entitled "Muslims Are Not a Race," in which he explains the dangers of categorizing Islamophobia as racism. Doing so, he writes, "turns Islam into a mere cultural marker of non-white people, a cipher that is spiritually, intellectually, and morally inert." Dagli's point is that if Islam is subsumed under the category of "race," the religion's majesty "becomes just one more social factor in a world where human affairs are reduced entirely to race, class, gender, and sexuality."

When I became a Muslim, I hadn't changed races; I adopted a set of beliefs that are largely misunderstood by the larger society, a reality that many Muslims misperceive as racism. As far as I was concerned, boiling down those beliefs to "non-white" diminished the power, heft, and possibility of what Islam offers America's fractured society.

As the lobster buckets fill, the entertainers for the evening file in carrying large African drums. From the minute I see the all-white musicians in their dashikis, I knew trouble would follow. By the time the band gets to their third song, a representative from the women of color section marches in, grabs the microphone at the front of the room, and begins to express their collective hurt over the cultural appropriation and the lack of diversity of the performers. I can see her first point, but as to her second, to be fair, we are in Maine.

She continues, "I just want to say that I am so angry and upset that after all the talking we have done today, we are still being appropriated and ignored!"

In tears, the white president of MANA clumsily rushes up to the microphone. "I am sorry!" she screeches, before choking up with anger, shock, humiliation, or all three. Composing herself, she goes on, "I am sorry for crying. And yes, these are my white tears! These are my white tears of apology. I tried, okay? I tried. I will keep trying."

My mustachioed neighbor shakes his head and clucks his tongue. I agree with his sentiment; I mean, what an embarrassment on all ends. I look at Sydney with eyebrows raised, and she meets my gaze, but not my gist. She's referring pointedly to the man next to me, while I'm baffled by the entire evening. But in that instant, I see through Sydney's eyes that my tablemate had transformed from a helpful neighbor to an angry right-winger who likely voted for Trump and perhaps even supported the Muslim ban. Division makes monsters of us all.

Like Sydney, many Muslims resonate with America's social justice movement and in fact see it as a contemporary expression of their faith's beliefs around justice. I've often argued to Sydney that, in their zeal for justice, Muslims adopt many of the movement's material solutions to what really is a spiritual problem. The Qur'an elegantly explains the nature and purpose of our varying hues, which, when applied, dispels any ideas of inferiority or superiority, "O humankind, We created you from a male and a female, and We made you races and tribes for you to get to know each other."

This room of segregated women and tone-deaf entertainment, in my eyes, represents the opposite of the Qur'anic mandate to allow your surface-level, skin-deep separation to bring you closer in understanding to one another. There is one American who grasped this Qur'anic concept. Once the conference is over, I catch a plane to go and visit him.

ഔ

We had reached the spot where the map indicated the grave would be, a small hill, the headstones laid flat so you could only see the names by walking directly up to them. A gravedigger sees our puzzled faces and my hijab and jabs his thumb toward a spot behind him; the only thing distinguishing it from the surrounding graves is a small brass vase with dried carnations rising above the ground.

I am moved by the humbleness of the gravesite. We settle ourselves on the damp grass next to the grave and greet the man we had come to see.

*Salam alaykum*, Al Hajj Malik al Shabazz.

Malcolm X. It's as if I could feel his lanky stature before me and that dazzling smile convey the salaams right back to me.

Sitting at his feet after the past couple of days, I feel a relief. Very few can understand the unusual journey of an American convert to Islam. Case in point, I don't think my grandfather would have imagined one of his granddaughters sitting at the grave of Malcolm X. And perhaps Malcolm couldn't have imagined me at his grave either. That's the thing about the path to God: it's beyond what we could ever imagine. Mine has led me here.

Malcolm's led him to Mecca, earning him the honorific title of Al Hajj, before his chosen Muslim name of Malik al Shabazz. In 1964, mere months before his life ended, Malcolm X traveled to Saudi Arabia to make hajj, the once-in-a-lifetime pilgrimage required of every able-bodied Muslim. In the now iconic trip, Malcolm, unaccustomed to seeing men and women of all races eat, drink, and pray together, has a revelation about race:

> During the past seven days of this holy pilgrimage, while undergoing the rituals of the hajj [pilgrimage], I have eaten from the same plate, drank from the same glass, slept on the same bed or rug, while praying to the same God—not only with some of this earth's most powerful kings, cabinet members, potentates and other forms of political and religious rulers—but also with fellow-Muslims whose skin was the whitest of white, whose eyes were the bluest of blue, and whose hair was the blondest of blond—yet it was the first time in my life that I didn't see them as "white" men. I could look into their faces and see that these didn't regard themselves as "white."

Here, on this patch of grass in New York, at the grave of a man Muslims consider a martyr who died for a noble cause, the desire to rectify America's racial sins, I feel my vision sharpen; from worlds apart, Malcolm and I came to view America through the lens of Islam. A man my parents and other whites of their generation feared saw Islam as the only viable solution for the race problem in America. And nearly sixty years later, having just attended a racially segregated dinner, I saw clearly that both sides of the racial divide are still in need of Malcolm's teachings.

We stayed with Malcolm, and his wife, Betty, until the edges of the sky tinged with darkness. Leaving Malcolm is a physical sensation, a goodbye to a presence, not to a decomposed body covered in dirt. It's like saying goodbye to a beloved grandparent, my cup now full, but the parting feels like a sharp yank. My tears don't stop until we reach the edges of the cemetery. We leave a different way than we came, but this time we don't need the map; the path is clear.

ॐ

Hafsa is already seven months pregnant when she and her husband Sulaiman ask me to be their midwife. Hiring a midwife later in the pregnancy can make for a short runway to get to know one another, but a few months earlier we had moved to the hills of Berkeley, the same twinkling hills I had arrived at sixteen years earlier. Zaytuna Institute had astonishingly gone from a yurt and a classroom to a thriving college in Berkeley, the first Muslim liberal arts college in America. Najeeb had begun working there some years ago, and we eventually moved into staff housing.

Hafsa and Sulaiman live in the apartment above us, so ours is an arrangement unusual for Bay Area midwives, who spend hours each day battling traffic to visit their clients. Midwifery has become a boutique and costly service in urban centers, one in which midwives call their moms "clients," and these clients "interview" several midwives before choosing the perfect fit.

Traditionally, however, each community had its own midwife, and the lives of the women she served were a mirror of her own. From her proximity, the midwife could keep a close eye on her expecting mothers, noticing subtle changes that might need attending to. Prenatal care as we know it today, with its measurements, labs, and ultrasounds, was at one time nonexistent, yet it existed in the sage observations of a midwife who would notice a mother slow to bring in her wash, which could indicate a need for more greens in her diet, or a mother with a pendulous uterus struggling to pick up her toddler, signaling a need for a scarf to support her growing belly as she went about her chores. The shared context of midwife and mother allowed for expertly made individualized adjustments, like when a seamstress responds differently to cotton than to silk.

In discussing the sacred dimension of craftsmanship in their book, *All Things Shining*, the authors Hubert Dreyfuss and Sean Dorrance Kelly acknowledge the importance of place and observation for the woodworker and his craft, which just as aptly apply to the midwife and her craft:

> The woodworker has an intimate relationship with the wood he is working. Its subtle virtues call out to be cultivated and cared for. This sense of intimacy with the wood initiates in the woodworker a feeling of care and respect for it. But it is not just the wood alone, as if it sprang fully cut and dried into his workshop. The wood has a place of origin, too, so the master becomes familiar with the local soil, the terrain, and the sources of water that nourish the trees.

Hafsa and I drink from the same well and gather produce from the same weekly farmers market, and from my second-floor window, I glow with pride as I watch Hafsa take off for a daily walk in the late morning sun.

A few weeks before her due date, some of Zaytuna's staff and students throw Hafsa a baby shower. There are a gaggle of little kids, some women who have never had a baby, and a few moms of young children. With three school-age kids, I feel like the wise old woman.

Our activity is to decorate birth affirmation cards for Hafsa to hang up and draw inspiration from during her labor. Birth affirmations are short and to the point, quickly read by a woman between contractions, or read to her by her support team, working by telling the brain what the body needs to know. *My baby knows how to be born. My body is healthy and strong. I have all the support I need.*

I choose to decorate the Qur'anic verse, *With every difficulty there is ease*, which I have always found so befitting to the rhythms of labor. Contractions last less than the space in between. And that space is nothing but ease to a sweaty mother. Penning carefully the English letters of this Qur'anic phrase, I feel an ease of my own—I belong here to these people, to this community of believers, and to the broader Bay Area community at large. Sixteen years ago, I had set off for California armed with little else but an intention to draw nearer to God and the teachings of his Final Messenger, and here I am surrounded by souls with the same goal. It has had its difficulties but, like the space between contractions, much more of the ease.

℘

Four months after converting to Islam, I visit my father before leaving for California, dragging the small U-Haul trailer full of books, a thrift-store coffee table, and my lime green Gary Fisher bike to his home outside of St. Louis. A couple of days before the journey, Darlene, whom I had met at the mosque, came to my studio apartment and spent several painful hours braiding my fine hair into neat cornrows. She told me that, since the extensions she used for my cornrows weren't my real hair, I would be excused if they stuck out of my beanie and a male saw them. Here I was, a white girl camouflaging her new faith with cornrows braided by a black woman guided by a questionable religious opinion. I'm still not sure how effective this was, but it relieved some of my anxiety about driving through America's heartland in hijab so soon after 9/11.

But I'm oblivious to my perplexed father's reaction; when he sees me in cornrows determined to leave the Midwest for a Muslim community in California, it nearly breaks him. I think it would have been easier on him had I come out as a lesbian.

His normally stoic face crinkles with worry as we sit down for lunch. "Are you sure, Shannon? I want you to be happy, but are you sure you're all right?" With one child freshly committed to a mental hospital, I'm sure he wonders if there will soon be two.

"Dad, I am so happy. Really, I can't imagine doing anything else. I feel more at peace than I ever have." I shake salt on my french fries and try hard to convey my newfound tranquility.

Before leaving town, I stop at the local mosque. Pulling a white polyester hijab over my braids, I climb the very narrow staircase to the cramped women's section. "Allahu akbar." I raise my hands to my ears as I say this and then let them hang at my sides. "Alhamdulillahi rabbi-l-alamin. Ar-Rahman Ar-Raheem. Maliki yaum id-deen. All praise to God. The most Merciful. The most Beneficent. Master of the Last Day." It's the first chapter of the Qur'an, the Opening, which is recited in each unit of the prayer.

After finishing the prayer, I carefully walk back down the steep, narrow steps when my nerves begin to catch up with me. What am I doing? How did I end up here, in a mosque? Where am I going? I had a prayer. Our Father Who art in heaven. Hallowed be thy name. Thy kingdom come; thy will be done. On earth as it is in heaven. What was wrong with my Catholic prayer? Quickening my pace, I try to cast this doubt from my mind. I've made my decision. And what I just told my father is true: I have never felt such a deep and abiding peace, even as I prepare to leave all that I've known, including a faith that I had never questioned.

At the bottom of the stairs, a wrinkled and worn sheet of paper is taped to the wall. I stop to read what it says. It's a type-written hadith, or prophetic statement. A providential message: *Actions are according to intentions, and everyone will get what was intended. Whoever migrates with an intention for Allah and His messenger, the migration will be for the sake of Allah and His Messenger. And whoever migrates for worldly gain or to marry a woman, then his migration will be for the sake of whatever he migrated for.*

Any doubts I had are quickly replaced by an enduring belief in God, the same God I had nightly prayed to my entire life, the same God I had sought out in frankincense-laden churches and while backpacking through canyons and forests—God is still my Sustainer. Who, aside from a loving God, would have directed my attention to this little piece of worn printer paper with words that have the power to transform the significance of the journey I'm about to embark on? I reread it through at least seventeen times.

Then, I pause and close my eyes. I make an intention as best as I know how. *O Allah, I am traveling to California with the intention to seek out You and Your Messenger. Please accept this from me.* With a steadied heart, I set my eyes on the western horizon and drive out of the mosque's parking lot.

ဆ

*With every difficulty there is ease.* I hand my card to Hafsa, and she shows me hers; it's the same exact verse, only done in beautiful Arabic calligraphy, a mirror of Arabic and English, a point reflection, an isometry of two surprisingly congruent shapes. Hafsa smiles her bright smile, her chocolate skin glowing from deep within. "You know what? I'm actually looking forward to the birth," she tells me. What more can a midwife ask for?

It is in this relationship between mother and midwife that I have surprisingly found my place. When the dynamics of distinguishing between a faith and an identity proved too much, like the woodworker who is focused in his workshop or the dad who escapes the cacophony of his family to tinker in the garage, it is to this sweet spot I would return.

Dreyfus and Kelly explain,

> Like any good relationship, each side brings out the other at its best. It is because the craftsman is an intelligent observer of wood and not a ruthless and unintelligible machine, that the wood can reveal to him its subtle virtues. But it is because the wood has these virtues already that the craftsmen can cultivate in himself the skill for

discerning them and ultimately can come to feel reverence and responsibility for the wood and where it lives.

Just as the wood helps to cultivate the craftsman, so the mothers whom I have served over the years cultivated me. Midwifery offered me a role and a purpose, one that I could not have found without being in relationship with the mothers I served. Just as a carpenter would cease to be without wood, a midwife needs mothers—their trust and gratitude proving to her that she is worthy of the title "midwife." When I may have fallen short of fitting in elsewhere, in the expectant space between me and a mother, there I belong.

Meanwhile, as Hafsa and I would learn, we come by this ageless relationship between midwife and mother naturally; it is nothing new to either of our family lineages.

Hafsa's mom, Khadija, has come to town for the birth. We are in Hafsa's sun-filled apartment as Khadija tells me about her own mother.

"She gave birth to five babies, all at home with midwives. This was Alabama in the fifties, the Jim Crow South. She used to tell me how the midwife would come to her and how she just somehow always knew when it was time to come. When the midwife saw that it was time for the baby, she would get my mother up on top of the bed."

My heart sinks, thinking that even then the midwives had adopted birthing practices designed for the hospital, moms on the bed while flat on their backs. But she goes on, "My mom had one of those old fashioned four-poster beds. The midwife would tie a sheet to the top of the post and have my mother squat right on top of the bed while pulling down on that sheet. My mom said it made those babies slide right out!"

It's heartening to know that women have good births in their families—your grandmother did it multiple times, so you can as well. The body's memory spans generations. When Hafsa's grandmother was squatting on that bed, pushing out Hafsa's mother, the egg that would one day become Hafsa was there too. We are a string, uncut back to our foremothers.

One recent summer, while sipping iced tea in the brick gazebo built by my grandfather, my maternal grandmother told me that her grandmother, my great-great-grandmother, was known as a midwife in her rural Iowa community. When the snow blew, she said, and the white icy drifts grew higher, people would say to the pregnant women, "Just call Annie Anderson; she's as good as the doctor." This work is in my body's ancestral memory too.

૬૭

Weeks later, I head up the stairs that separate my apartment from Hafsa's to check on her progress, or lack thereof. She is now two weeks past her due date, and nothing is working to coax labor. The smell of last night's spicy fried fish lingers in the air. The kitchen table cradles this morning's farmers market haul. Hafsa's belly is stubbornly unmoved.

# A Midwife's Search for Meaning

"I don't know when this baby is going to come! It seems like I'm going to be pregnant forever," Hafsa declares, her tall frame nearly swallowed by her swollen midsection.

It is said that while awaiting the Day of Judgment, souls will wait in anticipation for three hundred years. And that between the two blasts of the trumpet, signaling the end of the world, there will be forty years. That the angel's lips are already pursed upon the trumpet's mouthpiece.

Pregnancy and birth also do this to women; they warp and dilate time so that the last days of pregnancy can feel as long as the entire nine-month gestation, and one minute of a contraction can seem endless. When the baby arrives, its features are novel and unseen, yet a mother gazes into its face with instant recognition.

During birth, midwives too can experience a spiritual focus and elevation that takes them outside of time, as Dreyfus and Kelly describe,

> When we are the most excellent version of ourselves that we can be, when we are, for instance, working together with others as one, then our activity seems to be drawn out of us by an external force. These are the shining moments in life, wondrous moments that require our gratitude. In those episodes of excellence, no matter the domain, Odysseus's voice should ring through our heads: *"Be silent; curb your thoughts; do not ask questions. This is the work of Olympians."*

This work of sitting at the feet of laboring women, waiting on their waxing cervix, the immediacy of the moment drowning out the banal, the squalling wet life bursting into the room—these precious moments of walking the line between life and death contain a heightened awareness that supersedes any earthly concern. It is God's moment and He cares for all of His marvelous creation.

Later that evening, I am spooning Hafsa in her bed, my knees pushed into her back, providing counterpressure to the baby's occiput against her spine with every wringing of her uterus. As we awaken for each contraction and then slowly drift off between them, I think of our grandmothers—my great-great-grand-mother helping women in rural Iowa birth, perhaps just like this, her knees in their backs, helping them rest between contractions—and Hafsa's grandmother in Jim Crow Alabama, squatting with the help of a knowledgeable midwife to deliver her children. Yet here we both are, our paths converging at this geographic and historical point, the hills of Berkeley and the halls of America's first Muslim college. What may have seemed unlikely to our grandmothers is not.

This is why Malcolm's presence felt like home, and why the segregation of the midwives at the conference pained me, because there is another way to understand humanity's diversity than the simple one of skin color that we have been taught. We belong to God before anything or anyone else, and He has created our diversity so we may know one another and ultimately Him through His chosen palette.

Soon, we get Hafsa up. It's time to push. There is a pull-up bar in the kitchen. Sulaiman helps me to tie a sheet around it. Just like her grandmother before her, Hafsa instinctively reaches for the sheet, using it to descend into a deep squat. If birth is a reflection of culture, we have arrived at a new definition. I think Malcolm would be proud.

ᔥ

When I feel emptiest, the singularity of the path I've chosen rolled out ahead of me, with not even a forest to border or shade my walk, it is then that I think of Maryam. All alone during her time of need. Bewildered, in labor, thirsty and hungry. She had lived a life for God, and now she found herself in the difficult and humiliating situation of birthing a child without a father. Was this the thanks she got?

God didn't smooth the road for Maryam; He had prepared her for it. And in what must have been an immensely challenging trial for her, He didn't deliver her of her pain. He offered her dates and water, but also His presence.

"Do I have to shake the tree"? the Persian poet has her asking. I am so close to the Source, do I have still to work? But all you have to do is shake the tree; getting here was the hardest part.

"Another date?" Sulaiman offers. I thrust my hand into the sticky bag, a jumble of dates clumped together. My children are downstairs asleep. The teachers who have guided me through time and to this place are also asleep nearby, or perhaps they are awake and praying in the early morning hour. Hafsa is softly ac-quiescing to each contraction's squeeze. Sulaiman recites, *La il-laha illallah*, for the duration of each contraction. There is a cat mewing in the parking lot. I am so deeply at home. I must have shaken the tree.

"Sure," I say and pull out a juicy, plump date.

# EPILOGUE

Once again, I find myself at the foot of the teacher, only this time it's on Zoom, and instead of setting a wobbly foot in the swift and deep current of Islamic tradition, I am also imbibing my own Western tradition in the form of a book club. Arriving like an Eliza, all coarse manners and flowers, to Shaykh Hamza's Henry Higgins—language, and the art of arrangement—we read Aristotle, Jane Austen, Ibn Khaldun, Marcus Aurelius, Shakespeare, various English translations of the Qur'an, and more. Reading the Western classics with a man steeped in them who is also a scholar of the Islamic liberal arts provides a breathtaking interpretation that bends any boundaries that delimit where I belong—everywhere there is Truth, Beauty, and Goodness.

∞

Walking and running thousands of miles in the Berkeley hills during the global pandemic, I fielded questions about home birth from women afraid to enter hospitals who would have never before contemplated birthing at home; again and again I dispelled the common myths about the safety of home birth and affirmed their ability to birth their babies without any pain medication. While the media was adding up deaths, I was immersed in discussing life. As I ambled, the does bred fawns, eventually becoming young bucks with velvety horns that made the owners of small dogs cross the street. I watched the lavender wisteria vines bloom, only to give way to a riot of fuchsia bougainvillea followed by intoxicating and abundant rose bushes. My own children, too, sprouted amidst the Berkeley sun and the nurturing shade of Zaytuna's campus.

The years of the pandemic would prove to be my PhD in midwifery, as I attended nearly as many births in the three years of the pandemic as I had in the sixteen years prior. As the streets of downtown San Francisco, Oakland, and Berkeley succumbed to the fentanyl epidemic, their sidewalks devolving into a zombie apocalypse of abandoned addicts and human degradation, their tortured souls served to underline for me the centrality of family in society, and how protecting the very genesis of the families I was serving built a small bulwark against a rising tide of decay in a fractured and fraying country. Each new baby and its joyful parents represented a twinkling glimmer of hope, for as Plato says, "The beginning is the most important part of the work."

ॐ

One Ramadan, in the prayer room of Zaytuna's campus—a room grander than, yet not unlike, the small room I had sat in for classes when I first arrived at what was then Zaytuna Institute—Shaykh Hamza teaches a text on self-knowledge in the Islamic tradition by the twelfth-century Persian scholar Imam Raghib al-Isfahani. Taught in the hours before we break the fast, a time when the physical senses are dulled but the spiritual ones heightened, each class weaves a tapestry of the warp and weft of the human, from our basic biological and metaphysical similarities to minerals, vegetables, and animals, to the proclivities within our own souls that must be guarded against, to the heights of self-knowledge to which we can ascend, so elevated that some can surpass even the angels.

We finally arrive at the highly anticipated concluding chapter, the Gift of Death. This life, the one that I have spent decades watching come into existence, is allotted only a determined number of days—and when it reaches that final day, Imam al-Isfahani teaches us about the gift of its conclusion. Quoting a poet, he says, "The birth pangs of death came to him one day, and every pregnancy must complete its term."

Countless times I have watched a pregnant woman toil to bring forth the existence roiling in her uterus; pushing out, against all odds, around thirteen centimeters of a head, twenty inches of a body, and seven pounds of flesh always seems impossible, until it isn't. Once the mother has completed her pushing, I maneuver the baby through its cord, grabbing a warm blanket to dry off the remnants of the womb, and pass the already sonorous child to its mother. Everyone in the room blinks back tears; this place of birth is a union, and I believe when we see that moment, we are primordially reminded of our own impending reunion with our Creator, whose mercy is infinitely greater than even the mother who now weeps over the most precious thing to ever be placed upon her breast.

Imam al-Isfahani goes on to explain the poet's conceit, which is "to make death akin to the pregnancy of a woman, the pangs of death like the pangs of childbirth, and being born into another world, like the first birth, as a way of reminding us that this is one of the very purposes for existence itself." This is what I hoped to have gained from watching God's most marvelous act of creation again and again, to catch a reverse glimpse of death's inevitable landscape.

And to know with certainty that this abode is temporary and the creation of new eternal life easy for our Creator, or as Shaykh Hamza says in class, "We are in a cocoon. We are all caterpillars and death is breaking out of that cocoon to become a butterfly."

I pray that at the moment I expire my final breath, the awaiting of all of these first breaths has prepared me for my last. May that moment find me with the steadied, faithful heart of a midwife, one who, let it be known, has loved Allah and His Messenger ﷺ. May your last moment be your best, and in the next abode, may you be with those you love.

## ACKNOWLEDGMENTS

Thanks to God, our Creator and Sustainer, for our exemplar, the best of creation, our Prophet Muhammad ﷺ, who revered women and mothers. Bearing a book is akin to a gestation, and just as a human gestation brings out the best in others, so too has the carrying of this book. First to the teachers, those I know personally and those I don't, who have transmitted and exemplified our precious faith in this land. To Shaykh Hamza and Umm Yayha, there will never be enough thank yous to suffice for all you and your family have sacrificed and given, but thank you. Through Shaykh Hamza's aptitude for linking our Muhammadan inheritance to the greater liberal arts tradition, I've discovered richness and meaning in life's contractions and its ease. To Imam Zaid Shakir and Umm Hassan, reading Malcolm with Imam Zaid and the frank discussions about race that ensued confirmed for me the healing potential Islam can bring to our country. To Dr. Umar Faruq Abd-Allah, Dr. Sherman Jackson, Aisha Gray-Henry, and Shaykh Abdal Hakim Murad, your commitment to rooting Islam in the West helps me believe that a synthesis and creativity drawn from both heritages is possible. May the pure water of our faith continue to flow over and nourish these lands. To Hakim Archuletta, who gave me a crucial piece of advice at the very beginning of my midwifery journey, thank you. To Habib Umar, whose praise poem I use in chapter 6; Habib Ali; Ustadha Eiman Sidky; Usama Canon, may God have mercy on his soul; and Yahya Rhodus for preserving the spiritual traditions of Islam through your constant teaching and commitment to the prophetic way of life. To Feraidoon and Saima for teaching me that even the smallest details matter and that service is the highest form of worship. Feraidoon, thank you also for the poetic lesson on the embryo's journey down the fallopian tubes that begins this book. To Dr. Mohamed Boufares, thank you for reviewing chapter 6 and for your literary insights on writing about the *sirah* tradition.

To both Judys, Judith Tinkelenberg and Judy Luce, and Yelena Kolodji, I'm forever indebted to your thorough and detailed teaching and for keeping the art and science of midwifery alive for the next generation of women and babies. Many, many nights I have been alone at a birth and one of your voices would come to me from which I would find courage and a deep trust in a woman's ability to birth her baby. To my first midwife and mentor, Renee Anker, who encouraged me as a mother and midwife. To Lael, who proved to be the best midwife partner during a pandemic and beyond, but also an ardent supporter of my writing, giving me time off call and even traveling all the way across the country to give me a month to finish up this book. To Pearl, thank you for always being there for my midwifery concerns and questions, and then for always asking how my book was going once we solved said problem! To A'Maya and Eva for stepping in and holding down the practice as I neared the finish line.

To the Whitemans, Abdallateef, Tahira, and your brood, your encouragement, creativity, and humor have buoyed and inspired us. Thank you especially to Abdallateef for designing the logo and for your generosity in sharing your design wisdom. To Safir and Diane, thank you for reading early drafts of parts of this book and giving kind and considered feedback. To my in-laws, thank you Ammi, Abba, and Muniza for reading my drafts and for your support through all of these years, and Sami—who knew a midwife and author would need so much legal advice (thanks also to Tenaya for her legal counsel)! To Aisha, a light that arrived in my life when I needed it, for being one of my first and most encouraging and enthusiastic readers. To Mariam, for your pure love and bottomless talent, and as befitting to your magnanimity, thank you for not only the cover art but also the stunning cover design. To Nabila, for your support on this project, for always showing me that an examined life is the only kind of life, and for the honest advice, always. To Tyson Amir and Alia Mahmoud, for your enthusiasm about this book and all of the sage advice on self-publishing. To Elizabeth J. Asborno for her excellent copy editing, and to Rabia Spiker for her beautiful typesetting and independent publishing know-how. To Syeda Fatimah Hussayni, for graciously agreeing to proofread this book. To Jaime Fleres, who saw the potential in the seedlings of these stories so many years ago. Many others contributed in various ways, all of them appreciated, including Jon Eisenberg (what a good friend Najeeb has!), Carl Trueman (some of your ideas inspired chapter 5), Jeannette Cooperman, Kareem Salama (I have used your lyrics in chapter 6), Ayesha Mattu, Yusuf Mullick, Tom Devine, and Zak Whiteman. To everyone who replied with an "I can't wait to read it!" when I told them about this book, your enthusiasm and encouragement carried me like a swift Bay breeze.

To the mothers whose birth stories I've told, thank you for allowing me into your hearts and homes; you are forever in mine. To all the families whose precious birth stories are not included and whom I served along the way, there would be no midwife and no book to follow without your love, trust, and support. I am forever grateful to all of you.

To my father for inculcating a daily habit of reading, and the independence of thought that ensues, and to my mother for her acceptance of my chosen path. To Shawn, Melanie, Mackenzie and Mackoy, always in my heart. And an especially warm and giant thank you to Najeeb, Salek, Fatimah, and Ya Sin, who always made coming home, near.

www.ingramcontent.com/pod-product-compliance
Lightning Source LLC
Chambersburg PA
CBHW021717120626
46545CB00004B/1603